PRAISE FOR GOOD GIRLS GOSSIP

"We make life complicated and sometimes it is, but moments of childish happiness are the most precious of all. They make us feel young and alive, boosting our energy and self-belief off the scale. Thank you Tova. You say it brilliantly well. I love your beautiful book."

Edwina Dunn, CEO, founder of The Female Lead and author of *When She's In The Room*

"During a time when it feels like the entire world wants women to feel powerless, Tova reminds us that nothing could be further from the truth. The impact of a community of women coming together to share stories, spread joy, heal one another, and reignite internal fires that may have dimmed, is undeniable. Thank you for the inspiring, motivational wake-up call."

Danielle & Adam Silverstein, Founders of the Marriage and Martinis Podcast and Community

"Tova has written the perfect reminder that female strength lies in community and authenticity. Filled with real stories, practical exercises, and of course fun. Tova is so articulate yet so relatable. This book is for all women."

Jules Robinson, CEO, founder of Figure, TV persona, author and podcaster

GOOD GIRLS ~~DON'T~~ GOSSIP

TOVA LEIGH
GOOD GIRLS ~~DON'T~~ GOSSIP

Find Your Female Power

WATKINS
1893

For the women who have shaped me, supported me, and challenged me - whether for a moment or a lifetime. This book is for you.

This edition first published in the UK and USA in 2025 by
Watkins, an imprint of Watkins Media Limited
Unit 11, Shepperton House
89-93 Shepperton Road
London
N1 3DF

enquiries@watkinspublishing.com

Design and typography copyright © Watkins Media Limited 2025
Text copyright © Tova Leigh 2025

Tova Leigh has asserted her right under the Copyright, Designs
and Patents Act 1988 to be identified as the author of this work.

All rights reserved.
No part of this book may be reproduced or utilized in any form
or by any means, electronic or mechanical,
without prior permission in writing from the Publishers.

1 2 3 4 5 6 7 8 9 10

Designed and typeset by SJ Publishing Ltd

Printed and bound by CPI Group (UK) Ltd, Croydon, CR0 4YY

The manufacturer's authorised representative in the EU for product safety is:
eucomply OÜ - Pärnu mnt 139b-14, 11317 Tallinn, Estonia,
hello@eucompliancepartner.com, www.eucompliancepartner.com

A CIP record for this book is available from the British Library

ISBN: 978-1-78678-953-2 (Hardback)
ISBN: 978-1-78678-959-4 (eBook)

MIX
Paper | Supporting
responsible forestry
FSC® C013604

www.watkinspublishing.com

CONTENTS

Chain Smoking at the Kitchen Table   1

Not Quite Chapter One
Good Girls Gossip   7

Chapter One
Find Your Power Through Finding Yourself   19

Chapter Two
Find Your Power Through Giving Yourself Permission   41

Chapter Three
Find Your Power Through Addressing Your Needs   63

Let's talk about
Letting Go of Shame   77

Chapter Four
Find Your Power Through Playfulness   85

Chapter Five
Find Your Power Through Finding Your Wisdom   103

Chapter Six
Find Your Power Through Other Women   123

Chapter Seven
Find Your Power Through Pleasure   135

Let's talk about
Sexual Pleasure   145

Chapter Eight
Find Your Power Through Your Body 153

Chapter Nine
Find Your Power Through Doing Less 169

Let's talk about
Setting Boundaries 183

Chapter Ten
Call up the Girls 193

Notes 203

CHAIN SMOKING AT THE KITCHEN TABLE

I was 12 years old when I got my first period, and my mom told me, "You are now a woman." I remember walking around for a whole day looking at other women in awe. I felt special, like Wonder Woman with her cape and amazing hair. I wanted to put my hands on my hips and shout, "I am woman, hear me roar." It was as if I had entered a secret members' club of fierceness – like I had gone from being a little girl who cries when she scrapes her knee after falling off her bike to an Amazonian goddess who bleeds from her vagina and just gets on with it.

I couldn't put it into words, and this was not something my mother told me, but just by watching her with her girlfriends chit chat and chain smoke for hours at the kitchen table while us kids played outside, I knew there was something unique about their bond.

About women's bonds.

Something connected them which was more than the support they provided for each other with childcare and how they would look after each other's children when one of them had to run some errands, or how each day someone hosted lunch so that they didn't all have to cook every day (freaking genius if you ask me), or how they would borrow each other's clothes and kitchen appliances as standard.

It was cosmic.

When my mom was not with friends she often seemed sad and angry. I understand now that raising the three of us was no picnic, and that like many women she felt a sense of resentment because most of the household responsibilities fell solely on her shoulders. I also think that like many women she felt constrained by the stereotyped gender roles of her time and the expectations society had of her as to how she should behave as a woman, a wife and a mother.

But when she was with her girlfriends my mom would come alive. They all did. It was like the animalistic side of them that was dormant, and maybe even oppressed, would awaken. They brought out the best in each other and I would lurk by the kitchen door eavesdropping on their conversations and watching them laughing so loudly, wondering what the heck was so funny.

The way they would laugh when they were together was guttural and with their whole bodies. They crossed their legs so that they wouldn't pee, and with tears streaming down their faces they would grab each other by the arm and nearly pull one another off their chairs.

It wasn't polite or ladylike, it was big and wild, in the best way possible.

I know now that they understood each other like their husbands could never comprehend. Not many men can. I say this without judgement or resentment – after all, why should they be able to? It's not their reality or their experience. Funnily, I have come across quite a few men who rolled their eyes at me when I spoke of the female experience. They were unable to appreciate or accept the idea that it might be unique, that men's experiences in the world don't always match up to women's experiences. It's not surprising. The world is designed through the male experience and women are often an afterthought, meant to just get on with it. We see this in medicine, safety features on cars, and even the height and size of furniture – research and design are for and around men.[1] Because women are often looked at as a smaller version of men, many males find it hard to grasp that we think and feel very differently about our shared world.

When I watched my mother and her friends this was very clear to me. Like a pack of wild wolves howling with laughter at an invisible moon, I know now that what I was witnessing was their female authenticity, and it sparkled.

And I am not talking about "femininity" – which means different things to different people. For me it's not about the stereotypes, such as women being passive by nature, or the tropes that have women being nurturing and motherly, or even the fashion that says women have to have long hair or wear heels – or any of those things that over the years have become politicized and polarizing ("What type of woman are you?" type of thing). I'm talking about something more basic, something at our core that doesn't have a certain look, and is not based on any ideology. It truly is something we all share, whether we know it or not.

In those moments of joy, and sometimes moments of sorrow, my mother and her friends gave themselves permission to be totally genuine. They were able to shed their labels of "mothers", "wives", "good girls", "homemakers" and simply be who they were at their absolute core. Badasses, fierce, larger than life, brave, vulnerable, compassionate, rude, outrageous, ridiculous, thoughtful . . . human! The whole freaking shebang.

Like all women, they had shared experiences: heartbreaks, struggles, birth stories, aspirations, shitty bosses, health scares, culinary secrets, diet tips, diet struggles, diet hacks . . . basically lots of diet talk. They helped with each other's children, they gossiped and rolled their eyes about each other's men. They cried together, got angry together and they shared many of the same frustrations. As I got older I also came to learn that they often giggled about sex and toys, and they spilled the dirt on orgasms and favourite positions.

I didn't know what that was called at the time, and if I'm being totally honest it's taken me years to put a name on what that was. All I remember is feeling excited that one day I would be part of it. Some call it friendship, others call it a bunch of crazy women having a laugh, and some might have accused them of being bored housewives who drank too much coffee (or wine).

I call it female empowerment.

When you say "female empowerment" to people, many picture a bunch of angry feminists burning their bras and bad-mouthing men, and while there's nothing wrong with being an angry feminist and burning one's bra (or bad-mouthing men if they deserve it), that's not what "female empowerment" means to me.

It's also not entirely about confidence, or being assertive, or being able to publicly speak really well, or rock a bikini at any size, be authentic, prioritize your needs or embrace your body. I mean, sure, it's also all of those things, and self-acceptance is certainly a big part of it, but for me, at the core, female empowerment is something else.

It's that *togetherness* that my mom had with her friends. The camaraderie, the sisterhood, the pack culture.

It's that bond they shared as they chain smoked at the kitchen table with their big 1980s perms and chipped red nail varnish. The understanding without any effort. That magic that, at the same time, was totally earthy and grounded, which connected them and connects all women everywhere. It's a genetic memory, something in our ancient bones that we can't explain, or see or touch, but when we are together with other women we feel it and we know it's there. Even if just for a fleeting moment.

And that's the key – being together, being surrounded by other women, taking comfort from each other, learning from one another is what gives us permission to be ourselves. That's where the magic happens, in the connections we make with other women, in the bonds we have, in the unspoken understandings, shared wisdom and dialogue.

This wisdom, this something that has no name, can be tapped into at any given moment.

Many of us may have forgotten how, but it's easily remembered. We live in a world that has divided women –

by breaking down our commonality, our sense of community and our generational bonds, and also by prioritizing marriage over community – and by doing so has stripped us of our female power. That power of sisterhood and championing each other was replaced with isolation, mean girl culture and self-doubt – in order to diminish our place in society. For many women, female friendships are a threatening thought – that's something we talk about later – but they don't need to be.

That's why, throughout this book I will share the stories and journeys of some inspiring women I've had the pleasure of meeting throughout my life, as well as my own experiences and learnings. In sharing these I hope to encourage you to be more curious about the women in *your* life and entice you to seek out more female friendships and mentors, because I believe that when women come together incredible things occur, and I have seen this happen time and time again.

There is no need to take long courses, no need to read a million books on confidence, no need to spend lots of money or find gurus to teach you the secret to how this happens (unless you want to obviously). If you've picked up this book hoping it might help you find your female power, what you may discover by the end of reading is that this power is already within you. It's within all of us. When we come together and lift each other up, when we give ourselves and others permission to be ourselves, that's when the magic happens.

NOT QUITE CHAPTER ONE
GOOD GIRLS GOSSIP

"Gossip isn't scandal and it's not merely malicious. It's chatter about the human race by lovers of the same."

Phyllis McGinley

When I was eight years old, I had a fight with my best friend, Tamara. I couldn't tell you now what the fight was about, but I clearly remember feeling very frustrated about whatever it was we had fallen out over. On the way back from school the day we had our big argument, I was talking with another friend about it and sharing with her my frustrations and dilemmas, when her older sister, who was walking home behind us, said, "Good girls don't gossip."

I had never really heard that term until that day and I didn't know what it meant, but from how it was said I knew it wasn't a compliment. Tamara's sister obviously thought I was being mean. At bedtime, I asked my mother what "gossip" meant. She confirmed what I suspected, and told me that "a gossip" was someone who talked behind others' backs and usually said bad things about them, and that I shouldn't be one because it's not something "good girls" do.

I was confused.

How did sharing how I was feeling with a friend make me the villain? I understood why saying unkind things about other people wasn't a nice thing to do, but I didn't really see how trying to understand what had happened between me and my bestie, looking for wisdom, was so wrong. The whole thing gave me a strange feeling in my tummy. Like you feel when you're really hungry but you also feel a little sick at the same time.

Looking back, I know now that the feeling I was experiencing was isolation, and shame. It's lonely not being able to talk about what you're going through, and shame is a superb tool to keep people in check, particularly women. But I said nothing, I internalized it all and my biggest takeaway was that I should strive to be "good" – whatever the heck that meant.

But what if I told you that the word "gossip" originally meant something completely different to what it means today? What if I told you that the word was hijacked, that before it was turned into idle, backstabbing and catty girl talk or, as the dictionary has it, "to talk idly, mostly about other people's affairs",[2] it actually meant close female friends?

It doesn't sound so bad now, does it?

The roots of "gossip"

Bear with me as I talk a bit about history now, but I only recently discovered that the word "gossip" originates from Old English's "god-sibb" or "gods-sibling" which means godparents/god-relations – describing a close relation who acted as a "sponsor" at a baptism. By the time of Middle England, it had come to mean the women who helped other women before, during and after they gave birth, essentially midwives,[3] which then simply came to mean "a close female friendship" – i.e. those with whom you would "gossip" at "friendship meetings" – leading to the verb "gossip" to mean close conversation: "Gossip came to denote women's friendships which, in the time leading up to the 1500s [in England], were particularly strong and held importance in public life."[4]

Like the boys with their "locker room talk" or "gentlemen-only members' clubs" where they smoked cigars, sipped brandy and talked politics, women had their "gossip", which basically meant getting together to tell stories, solve problems, laugh, process, get advice, offer empathy or just listen . . . you know, to be there for each other in a way that was integral to forming communities.

This is not a history lesson, but around the 17th century, the interactions and friendships amongst women began to be demonized – Puritanism was rife, and with it the judgement of others for women's perceived moral lack. Women were deemed inferior to men, and more susceptible to temptation from the devil.[5] You see, "gossip" assisted women in creating close connections and networks, independent of men, which have always been a source of female power. And as women gaining power independently of men was seen as a threat to the male-dominant society, by the 17th century the term "gossip" had evolved to become a way to mock and degrade women, their words, their ways of sharing information, and their supportive bonds.

In the 18th century, women who "gossiped" were put into muzzles that prevented them from speaking – a "scold's bridle" or "gossip's bridle" was introduced by the church.[6] Far from speaking ill about others, women were prevented from simply speaking *at all*. That's how afraid society was of women and their collective power. Preventing women from "gossiping", or labelling their conversation as "tittle-tattle", was a way to divide women and strip them of their greatest strength.

So basically over time the word gossip changed in meaning and morphed into what we know today – talking sh*t about someone behind their back. Labelling women talking with other women (and those who did so) as "idle" was a misogynistic tool to oppress and silence them, and ultimately strip women of their power. And in case you're wondering what power I am referring to, well that's easy – the power and strength of the female community. The sisterhood. The togetherness which I will keep banging on about throughout this book.

Silence them

Throughout history women were builders of communities. Natural communicators whose biggest strength has always been the bonds and networks we build through our relationships with other women. Yet, women's voices have been seen as a threat to the status quo in patriarchal societies and unfortunately elements of the desire to silence women still exist today in some parts of the world. In 2024, the Taliban banned Afghan women from speaking or singing along with showing their faces in public.[7] Women's voices have also been banned from radio or TV broadcasts in some regions. Just as in 1547, when a proclamation was made "forbidding women to meet together to babble and talk", requiring men to "keep their wives in their houses".[8]

Over the years the idea of gossip being a negative thing, usually associated with women, was reinforced. But it was much more than criticism about talking negatively about other people behind their backs. It was a disparagement about women (specifically) talking, period. From Jane Austen and Shakespeare to *Mean Girls* and *Gossip Girl*, the association between gossip and gender in society is deeply embedded – a disparaging, demeaning and belittling connection.

The idea that women talk a lot and that much of what we say is trivial and unimportant – as opposed to men who say less, but when they do weigh in, everyone should listen because it must be very important – seemed to be a general consensus. Women are commonly portrayed as overtalkers and oversharers who engage in dangerous, damaging and/or unimportant chatter – a message reinforced in movies, the media, literature and even everyday language with proverbs and old sayings from across the globe: "Women's tongues are like lambs' tails – they are never still" (Old English saying), or "Nothing is so unnatural as a talkative man and a quiet woman" (Scottish saying), or "One man, one word – one woman, one dictionary" (German saying) and "Where there are women and geese, there's noise" (Japanese saying).[9]

Jokes are even made about how much women talk – we've all seen the "humorous" greetings cards with a caricature of a woman talking *at* their husband who has long since died yet the wife is still mid-sentence, and the like. You may have also heard the "fact" that women say more words per day than men do. This statistic was cemented in the original edition of *The Female Brain,* published in 2006, in which author Louann Brizendine, MD claimed that women speak around 20,000 words a day, while men only say around 7,000.[10] It soon became the pearl of wisdom everyone would quote at dinner parties, and let's face it, how can someone possibly say three times more than men do and have all those words be important, right? The only possible conclusion therefore was that women simply don't shut up and that most of what we say is utter toss or . . . gossip.

The interesting thing about the above "fact" is that it wasn't actually based on any real research. It was an urban myth.[11] There have been a raft of sobering studies into the relative speaking times of men and women in a range of professional and personal settings and they make for uncomfortable reading. Overwhelmingly women fail to produce the expected amount of speech relative to men that you would assume based on the women/men ratio in a group, and are often talked over/disadvantaged by attempts to put forward opinions.[12]

Unfortunately the consensus remains that women talk so much more than men (with the implication that this extra wordage is superfluous at best), which of course is ironic given how, in reality, women are so often silenced by men. As academic and keynote speaker Dale Spencer explains: "The talkativeness of women has been gauged in comparison not with men but with silence. Women have not been judged on the grounds of whether they talk more than men, but of whether they talk more than silent women."

From classrooms, where female students are known to say less than male students,[13] to the movie standard of male actors having more lines than their female co-stars,[14] as well as boardrooms, news panels and even online. Let's face it, no one seems to like a woman with a lot to say.

It was never about stopping women from saying bad things about other people; it was always about not wanting women to say anything at all. It was about removing the power of talking with each other as a group. This powerful and necessary tool for communication, sharing of information, story-telling and community-building became a tool for oppression – the term weaponized against women.

Talking is good

Most "gossip", of course, isn't even negative, and it's a natural thing. We all talk about other people and most of the time we don't actually say bad things about them. Don't get me wrong, I am not saying women *never* say unkind things about others – of course we sometimes do – what I *am* saying is that many times when we speak about others we do so as a way to reflect on our own lives.

We use our peers' stories and experiences as inspiration, we learn from their mistakes and successes, we compare their life choices to ours as a way to assess our own lives, and often we talk about other people because we are worried about them and we care. Telling stories (about events as well as other people) is also a vital tool to pass down information and history and keep memories of those who have passed alive.

On top of that, chatting amongst friends is actually a very healthy thing to do. Speaking to friends often relieves stress, depression and generally makes you happier. Some say that women having more meaningful friendships that involve more chit chat compared to men is possibly one of the reasons why women live longer than men do.[15] Women gather together in times of crisis, we seek each other out, we take comfort from one another and we offer a listening ear.

But beyond that, venting to someone close about what's bothering you, about behaviour that impacts on the social structure around you, even if it involves talking about someone else, enables you to explore your own life choices and how they make you feel, and supports you in feeling less alone. I saw this from my own experience, but I am sure this is true for others too. And while not all "gossip" is kind, and not all of it should be promoted, it is through "gossip" that women have mastered and value the power of empathy and the understanding of the suffering of others.

Embrace gossip

There is a lot to be said about collective wisdom, and every woman you meet has wisdom to share. And when I say "wisdom" I don't necessarily mean knowledge or skills you might learn at school or university. Those are also great and many women can share their professional and academic knowledge, for sure. But what I am referring to is the type of wisdom that comes from life experience. Stories, understandings, insights and even intuition. I believe that when there is a will for dialogue then there is potential for learning and we all have something to teach, just like we all have something to learn.

When I started running female empowerment retreats a few years ago I made this very clear from the start. Most of the participants still find that surprising, because they initially come to the retreat with an intention to learn either from me or from the other facilitators I've sourced. But the truth, as they very quickly discover, is that the learning *from each other* is far more profound and meaningful. And that makes me so happy. We have a wealth of wisdom inside us and when we have the right space to share it with other women, miracles happen.

We can also learn a lot from stories about other women.

While I am by no means in favour of cruel and malicious conversations about other people behind their backs, I do believe that it is *not* what takes place in most cases when women congregate. So, if you're having a mixed reaction to the word "gossip", I get it. But for the purpose of this book, I ask you to put aside your preconception and entertain the idea that reclaiming "gossip" is necessary – not just as a term but also for women as a platform for self-expression and to enable us to form deeper bonds with each other.

In this book, I invite you to "gossip" with me about some of the incredible women I have met along the way, whose stories have inspired me and touch on the themes of the book: from permission and boundaries to pleasure, doing less, and wisdom. I also share my own experiences to demonstrate how we are all each other's teachers and how it is through our relationships with the other women in our life that we grow and better ourselves, that we access our female power. I think we can never celebrate the women in our life enough and I hope that's something you take away with you. Shout about the brilliant women in your life, and hopefully they will do the same for you!

Throughout the book I will also introduce the exercises and tools that have helped me with my own journey to finding my power as well as practices and prompts that will help you apply the ideas in the book. While you may have picked up *Good Girls Gossip* in the self-help section, please remember that I am not a therapist. I'd like to think of us as a tribe and myself as one of the tribe elders who is sharing her life experience with other women. It might sound silly but I love the idea of women sitting around a fire sharing their life stories, gossip and tips and tricks that worked for them.

Each chapter is like a piece of a puzzle or a roadmap to finding your power. These tools and practices come from the worlds of physiology, wellness, spirituality and even the performing arts from my days as an actress. I've had a keen interest in many of these topics for many years and have participated in various women's circles, workshops and I even run my own female empowerment retreat. Not everything

I suggest will be your cup of tea, but I encourage you to approach all with an open mind and heart as their impact may surprise you.

I know this can sound a bit of a cliché but I'm going to say it anyway because I'm a sucker for a cliché – this book is for *you*. Not for anyone else, just you. If you're anything like I used to be – as with so many women – you probably do so much for everyone else, yet very little for yourself. While many other people in your life are undoubtedly important, the truth is that *you*, and just you, are the most important person in your story. You are the leading lady of your own life!

I can't promise to give you all of the answers, but remember that sometimes asking the questions is more important than the answers themselves.

Let's "gossip" about Vanessa...

I met Vanessa through work. She was a columnist for a lifestyle magazine in Portugal and we met and instantly clicked. She is an impressive woman with a fascinating background in journalism, languages, travel and charity work, on top of being a wife, mother and the head of her kids' school's PTA. Vanessa is one of those women you look at and think, "Wow, she's really got her sh*t together."

We saw each other for the occasional lunch or dinner with cocktails and I invited Vanessa on a retreat with me. She was delighted to accept and so I got to spend five days and six nights with her outside of our usual surroundings.

On the first day I guided the group through an improvisation workshop. If I were to describe what people do in these workshops in the simplest way I would say — play like little children!

Vanessa loved it. She was giggling throughout the workshop and by the end of it there were tears of joy streaming down her face. I could tell that a part of her that was dormant had awakened and over the next few days she continued to shed her professional persona and evolve into someone who was free, spontaneous, whimsical and utterly bonkers.

By day three Vanessa had let her hair down from her usual tight ponytail — literally and figuratively — her long blonde hair was blowing in the wind as she swung on a big swing hanging on one of the trees in the garden. "Take a picture of me," she yelled as she went higher and higher.

She was beaming.

Before we left after the retreat was over, she thanked me. "I haven't laughed this much for years. Thank you for reminding me that deep down I am still that little girl who loves swings. I've missed her."

I didn't expect it ahead of the retreat and this was by no means my plan, but I basically got to meet Vanessa without her different hats on. Not the career woman, not the wife or mother, not the incredible organizer, not the superb cook or responsible parent...just Vanessa — the girl behind all the labels.

CHAPTER ONE
FIND YOUR POWER THROUGH FINDING YOURSELF

I invite you to think about the idea of "finding yourself" for a moment. What comes to mind when you hear the phrase "find yourself"? What type of words come to you when you think about describing who you are? Take a moment and make a list of the words, phrases or ideas. Now read the words you wrote down and notice how they make you feel. Does it feel like a complete list? Are there words that you dislike? Was this a challenging task or did you find it surprisingly easy? Try to let go of any judgement you might have about what you are writing. This is a private exercise, no one needs to know what you've written, it's just for you to observe.

Most people when asked who they are list their name, qualifications, job descriptions, marital status, parental status, age, nationality, religion, etc. We are used to telling people about ourselves in terms of our labels – when meeting someone at a party, or talking about ourselves at job interviews and on our résumés. Even our names are labels that can be changed. Dating sites ask about our hobbies and lifestyle choices; our social media profiles give us categories to choose from.

As humans our nature is to catalogue things. We like having things sorted into boxes, it helps us understand the world better and make sense of the chaos, but it's potentially detrimental when we apply this logic to ourselves. I am pretty sure I used "I need to find myself" several times in my 20s (and 30s) when I was in the process of shedding the old me and discovering who I was going to become in the next chapter of my life. Up until my early 20s, I lived at home with my parents, and most of my identity was tied to the role I played in my family. I was the eldest, the one who followed the rules, the "good girl". I don't think I had a strong sense of who I was outside of that framework. Then, in my early 20s, I moved out to attend university, and for the first time, I was truly on my own – free to figure out my own place in the world. I met people who approached life in ways I'd never considered, who held different political views, read books I'd never heard of, and challenged the way I saw things. It was a time of self-discovery, of uncovering who I was beyond the expectations I'd grown up with.

Transitions

If I am being totally honest, I never really stopped to think about "finding myself". I didn't wake up one morning and say "gotta find myself", nor did I wonder if I never knew myself to begin with. It sort of happened organically because I made a change in my life. Some of my friends travelled to the Far East to "find themselves" – they did this through experimenting with drugs, living alternatively, connecting with nature and meeting lots of different people from all over the world; even though there wasn't any manual of how or why one would "find themselves", somehow what they were doing totally made sense to me.

For me the need to "find myself" has always been sparked by change. Usually a change in my circumstances – like moving out of my parents' home to go to university, or getting married, getting a divorce, becoming a mother, the kids growing up, etc. Every time something major like that happened in my life, I felt the need to redefine myself. To discover once again who I was or who I was becoming.

Transitions are hard. Especially when we feel we are transitioning from one version of ourselves into another. The most obvious transition I can think of, one which we will all go through, is the aging process. No matter what we do, how well we eat, sleep and workout, we will all age and there is nothing we can do about it. Every age brings with it new roles for us to play in our own and in others' lives. When we are young, we are daughters and friends. We later become lovers and mothers. And as we mature some of us step into our power as queens and wise women, all feminine archetypes. I have in certain points of my life found it hard to transition from one role to another and have often felt a deep sense of sadness about leaving certain parts of me behind.

There is also how society looks at women to take into account here. For example, while certain roles like "mother" are celebrated, other roles like "wise woman" are not. As a society it seems that we prefer our women forever young – attractive and naive, so for many women the idea of getting older is very threatening. As women age we are able to tap into our wisdom more, trust our instinct, listen to our gut and also not be so afraid or worry about what others might think about us. Which means that we say stuff that pisses people off. On the one hand, it's a liberating stage of life, but on the other hand, it also comes with a price.

Transitions, whether in careers, relationships or personal growth, can feel overwhelming. If this is how you feel about them, then try to reframe transitions as dynamic and evolving rather than as a definitive "end" to make them less intimidating. This perspective allows you to honour what came before, while also moving toward the new you – it's not about abandoning who you were but carrying forward those elements that align with who you're becoming.

Losing ourselves in childhood

When we are born we are pretty much a clean slate. As children, we're as close as we'll ever get to being untouched by external influences. It's like Play-Doh that has never been touched. Maybe that's why watching kids interact is so captivating – they're a reflection of raw authenticity. Everything is fresh to them. There's no baggage, no reference points, just honest, unfiltered reactions.

As children, we observe our surroundings and often learn how to behave by watching how adults react to situations. The best example I can give you is when my daughters were younger they were dancing to Madonna's "Get Into The Groove" in the living room and one of them tripped over a toy and fell. I resisted the urge to immediately jump up and make a fuss because it wasn't a big fall and I wanted to see how she reacted before making an assumption, so I simply observed her reaction. The first thing she did was look around to see if anyone had seen her fall. It was almost as if she was checking the world's reaction to what had happened to her, perhaps to establish how she should feel about it. She then caught my eye and I smiled at her. She smiled back, shrugged her shoulders, hopped back up and carried on dancing with a massive smile on her face. I found the whole event fascinating and I couldn't help but wonder what she would have done if I had seemed worried or made it into a bigger deal.

A few years later, we were at a friend's birthday party and the kids were playing football with the dads in the garden. One of the little boys was hit by a ball which knocked him over and he started to cry. His dad encouraged him to get right back up and shake it off. His mother watched from afar, smiling and gave him a thumbs up. A few minutes later nearly the same exact thing happened, only this time it was a little girl who was hit by a ball and had fallen over. Her father gave her a big hug and asked her if she wanted to sit out for the rest of the match. Her mother ran over, looking worried, and after a short discussion she came off the pitch and was given ice cream to make her feel better. I watched the whole scene play out and pondered on how differently we treat boys and girls, and how this early conditioning impacts us as people throughout our lives. What does it teach us about our place in the world, what we can handle, what the world's expectations of us are and just generally how it shapes us?

What I am trying to say is that how we feel about things and our reactions to events are often a reflection of how the world sees us. From an early age we are "told" who we are, what we are like, what our strengths and weaknesses are, what we are good at, and what we should do when we are older. Also how we should behave, dress, express ourselves, and interact with others, and what should be important to us.

Both directly and indirectly, we are told our role in the world. Society treats us in a certain way depending on the colour of our skin, social class, gender, physical appearance, sexual orientation and so on. Our views on everything – from career choices to political leanings – are impacted by where we grew up, what our parents' beliefs were, what we were taught at school and more. And all of that feeds into who we are, which is why answering the question "Who am I?" is very complex.

Many women I've spoken to have shared with me that they don't know who they are. They expressed that they feel they have *lost* themselves, either to motherhood or marriage, or because of changes to their bodies, careers, etc. Some said they weren't sure they knew themselves to begin with. That for their whole lives, or at least from the point they could remember, they felt like they were playing a part. Acting a role for someone else. It could have been the role their family expected them to play, their partner, or even society, which led them to waking up one morning and realizing they had no idea who they were. I don't think this is surprising and I can certainly relate.

Losing ourselves in mothering

As women we hold many roles in society – from community leaders to businesswomen – and also we traditionally act as the primary caregivers in the family, often responsible for caring for elderly parents, the kids and looking after the home. While customary gender roles have been challenged more recently, and changes have occurred, with more men participating in childcare and the domestic chores, women carry more of this burden and so our roles as caregivers and mothers are fully entwined with our sense of identity.

Mothers and carers are generally held to higher standards than fathers. They are expected to do more, sacrifice more, dedicate more time, be more present and involved, which all contributes to the reason this role becomes an identity for many women that often defines us. It frequently becomes the *main* role women play (or are expected to play for those who choose not to or do not have children), whether they want to or not, and this is a result of many factors, from gender stereotypes in our society to financial reasons.

If we asked our mothers, grandmothers or other women in our families we might discover that women's loss of identity is often generational. How many of us truly see our own moms as the women they were before they became our mothers? Who were they before they became the people who dropped us off at soccer or music practice or cooked all our meals for us? What hobbies did they have? What were their values and dreams? What inspired them or made them laugh? Who are they apart from "mom"?

Losing ourselves in marriage

Losing our sense of who we are is also easy in marriage and relationships. There is a natural impulse, arguably stronger for women, to please those we love and so many of us find ourselves losing autonomy in our relationships in order to have "harmony", to compromise and not rock the boat.

Historically, a woman's identity was linked (legally and socially) with the men in her life, to the point that she didn't exist independently – firstly to her father then a male spouse. "Coverture" was a legal practice (part of our colonial heritage) in which women and their children had no legal identity (based on the French word *couverture* to mean "covering"). It was established in the common law of England, and practised for several centuries through to the end of the 19th century. According to this practice, when a girl was born she was covered by her father's identity, and then when she was married, by her husband's identity. Once married, a couple's identity merged into one: the husband's. Married women could not own their own property, nor were they allowed to enter a contract themselves or own a business (or to sue anyone).[16]

Obviously times have changed and today in most parts of the world women can work, vote, own property, enter contracts themselves and decide whether or not to take their partner's name (should they wish to get married) – but many of these developments were relatively recent. For example, in the US, banks required single, widowed or divorced women to have a man cosign any credit application up until 1974, regardless of their income. In the UK, women could legally be refused the right to drink in a pub unaccompanied by a man up until 1982.[17]

I believe that a genetic memory of a time in which women were seen not as individuals but rather as a part of someone else's identity is still consciously and subconsciously impacting women today. Even in 2024, although more and more women opt to stay single/unmarried and/or childless, there is still pressure on women to "settle down". Adopting an identity as wife and mother is promoted – in the movies we watch, the media and advertising we consume, and the general consensus of society.

These roles we take on also impact our relationships with other women. Yes, we share the negative impacts of these roles and the obligations associated with them, but there is a sense of competition which often isolates us, or leaves us in a place where we judge/compare ourselves to the women around us facing the same challenges, just when we need to be surrounded with and supported by women the most. The most obvious example that comes to mind is dating and mating – two girls fighting over a boy is one of the main narratives in so many stories and movies. *My Best Friend's Wedding*, *Bride Wars*, and *Gone With The Wind* are just a few examples. Even with 1980s female pop stars – you were either team Madonna or team Cyndi Lauper, you couldn't be both. I certainly grew up feeling that there were fewer great guys than there were great girls and so the competition was on! Now, with more women financially secure and with a greater freedom in terms of careers, fulfilling our ancestral conditioning of "mating up" is getting harder and harder and a reason why so many women are opting to not marry or settle down at all. But for those who remain in the race, it's truly a brutal one.

The other obvious example is motherhood, when the sense of competition between moms is undeniable: who is doing more, whose kids are achieving what, who is making homemade natural protein balls at 5am in the morning while maintaining a spotless home with recycled wooden toys and zero use of screens. The pressure is on and it divides mothers into subgroups. There used to just be stay-at-home mom vs working mom but now you have a whole list of sub-categories: from the Pinterest Mom effortlessly whipping up hand-sewn costumes and themed birthday parties that belong in a magazine, to the Helicopter Mom, who's always on high alert and ready to swoop in with hand sanitizer and a backup plan.

Motherhood is becoming another way for women to show each other up rather than something we bond over. The point that I am trying to make is that while categories are meant to help us figure out who we are, what they often do is restrict us and force us to choose one thing over the other. Seeing who we are through the lens of a drop-down menu lacks nuance and ultimately doesn't work when it comes to describing humans (and even less so when you try to sum up women because let's face it we are so wrongfully complex).

Not knowing

Not knowing who you are is a challenge to finding your power. There can be judgement or shame around feeling lost in the roles held by a woman. But how does one even approach this question, especially when it can mean so many things?

I noticed a few years ago that when facing the question "Who am I?", I used to list all the things I was *for others*. Someone's mother, someone's wife, coworker, sister, friend . . . I didn't really have a sense of anything else, separate from other people, it was always in relation to someone else. When I look back I can't tell when this happened. When I was a little girl I was told to be a "good girl", to be considerate, to help my mom and look after my siblings, and somehow throughout my upbringing, like many women of my generation, I learnt that my job was *to do for others*. Does that sound familiar? Could that perhaps explain why so many women feel they have lost themselves?

It didn't bother me until my early 40s when it became clear to me that I had no idea who I was anymore. Who I was under all the labels, beyond the responsibilities and other people's expectations, free from how others saw me or what they wanted me to be like. You see, we had three kids in the space of two years. Before that, I was a working actress. It never paid the bills but it fed my soul, and performing was a big part of my identity. Then after becoming a mother, I stopped acting because motherhood took precedence, my entire world had become about meal plans, mashed bananas, school runs and eating the kids' snacks while hiding in the pantry on the verge of having a nervous breakdown, and when I looked in the mirror I simply had no idea who I was anymore, apart from being an absolute wreck.

Even my first name had been replaced with "Mom" and as much as I loved being a mother, it felt like everything else about who I was had vanished. I would use external components like my job, education, religion, marital status, etc, and of course how others perceived me, to define myself. But actually there were many internal components I wasn't really considering at all. Like how *I* saw myself. What type of person am I on the inside? What are my thoughts, beliefs, values? Was I kind, thoughtful, moody? Did I do the right thing, was I vindictive, happy, full of joy or perhaps resentment? Some of these things are determined by how we think and some are determined by our actions. And sometimes there is a conflict between these aspects.

After my "midlife crisis" in my early 40s (which I wrote about in my book *F*cked at 40*), which prompted me to reconnect with sides of me that I felt I had lost and discover who I was apart from being something for others, I felt like I had found myself again. (By the way, I use quote marks because in reality it wasn't a midlife crisis at all but more of an awakening. I use the term just because it's more familiar to people.) For a few years, whatever definition I had found felt suited and very comfortable, but then toward my late 40s I started feeling restless again. When people ask me "Who are you?" now, I simply can't put it into words at present. While in the past I felt the need to reclaim parts of me that I had lost, now what I need is to not be restrictive. The new me is many things. The new me can't be described in a list. The new me is always evolving and changing and I am okay with that.

No limits

I was taught to think in terms of "black and white". Many of us were. You're either in or out, good or bad, a fairy and love unicorns or a superhero and into cars. You can't be both. The world is often presented to us as binary with two opposing options to choose from – good/bad or right/wrong – and this narrative is reinforced in literature, social media and movies. We grew up watching films with "goodies" and "baddies". Fairytales and folk stories tell of evil vs good. The word "or" often shapes how we perceive and process the world.

For years I had the habit of living with such limited and narrow options, which felt very restricting and also put a lot of pressure on me to get things right. There was no flexibility or "grey" areas, there was just a right or wrong answer and I had to make the correct choice. This restrictive approach to myself, my preferences, interests and abilities showed up in many places in my life, but the best example is probably my choice of career.

Growing up, I was always told I would make a great attorney because I was a good talker. My analytic and academic abilities were praised, while my creative side was ignored. I subscribed to the narrative that you can only be one or the other – an academic *or* a creative. So I took the path everyone seemed to think was best suited for me and got a BA degree in both Business and Law, passed the Bar exam and even practised law for two years before deciding to ditch it all and become an actress! Funny enough these days I use *all* the skills I have to do my current job.

My day job is a blend of creativity and business. It's not about one *or* the other – it's a combination of different things, much like life often is.

WHO SAID YOU HAD TO CHOOSE?

So I learnt a new trick – I started replacing the word "or" with the words "and also". I know it sounds silly, but you will be amazed by how powerful this practice is! I basically exchange the word "or" with "and also" and allow myself to be/feel multiple things and not have to choose one camp over another. It meant moving away from a binary way of thinking toward a more holistic approach. Because when you think about it, most things in life are actually not white or black. There are many shades of grey, but as humans we feel uncomfortable in the uncertainty so we rush to choose. Saying "and also" is a form of kindness we show ourselves in those moments.

Suddenly I was able to be a good mother *and also* a mother that hated arts and crafts and sometimes wanted to escape her kids. I was able to be a loving wife *and also* question if marriage was ever for me. I was able to be a performer who gets up on stage and makes people laugh *and also* a video creator who talks about serious stuff like sexism and gender stereotypes. In other words, I was able to see myself as more than one thing or another, even when those things were seemingly contradictory.

I invite you to play with this tool and think about the different ways you can use it. Think about the areas in your life in which you use the word *or* and try to replace it with *and also*. How does that make you feel? Are you an introvert *and also* someone who needs more community and support? Are you adventurous and love experiencing new things *and also* have anxiety and sometimes want to hide in your room? Do you love being a mother *and also* really hate it sometimes? Are you creative *and also* have an analytic brain?

This tool can be used in any area of your life – from motherhood to your choice of career or friendships or even when talking about your personality traits. The point is to start looking at yourself in a more holistic rather than a binary way. Things don't have to be black and white, there is a lot of kindness, freedom and honesty in the shades of grey – why not allow them into your life?

Self-acceptance

And what if we give ourselves permission to not know?

When I asked my 12 year old, "Who are you?" she said "I don't know yet." I found it refreshing that not knowing didn't bother her, but I also found it very interesting that she assumed she would one day know.

What if we never have a coherent answer? What if who we are is a work in progress and so we never quite arrive at a station in which we can declare to the world, "This is who I am!" because we are constantly changing?

When I say find your power through finding yourself I don't mean that you have to have everything figured out.

When I looked at myself in the mirror all those years ago and could not recognize who was standing in front of me, the first impulse I had was to judge myself. How could I lose myself so badly? How did I let this happen? How did it come to this, and how could I fix this as fast as possible? I jumped into action in an attempt to regain all the parts of me I felt I had lost, and it helped a lot, don't get me wrong. I made a bucket list which included things like bungee jumping, a trip to Nepal, taking up pole dancing, doing a nude photoshoot, etc. And through all these things I found my sense of adventure again, I reconnected with my body and sexuality, and I felt more like myself over time. It wasn't necessarily about getting my "old self" back, just the parts of her I missed and knew were still in there. It was more about uncovering "new" elements of my current self – the new and improved model.

But looking back, I know now that what helped me more than anything else was something a friend said. She said, "I know you want to find the old you again and get her back, I know you feel like you don't know who you are and like you've lost yourself, but just know that this version of you, this version right now, is also great, just the way you are."

Just the way you are

How often do we allow ourselves to consider that the current version of ourselves is just fine? It helps to understand that things about us can be temporary and not fixed in stone. Whatever you are feeling, or whoever you are at any given moment, doesn't have to define you for life.

When we don't know who we are or accept who we are, it is very difficult to acknowledge our needs, or to see why they are important and worth our attention. If I am no good as I am, my needs will be the last thing that I will respect or focus on, as I will be too busy trying to either punish myself or fix myself to be better, while focusing on other people's needs.

It's great to say "just be yourself" but if we don't at least accept who that is, how are we ever going to give ourselves permission to do it in the first place?

When I started my own journey one of the challenges I had was to accept myself as I am.

This was not easy because of my own perception of myself. You see, I had thought for years that I was "bad". That under all the layers I was not a good person. That even though I did good things and behaved in a way that is considered "good", I was convinced that this was not the real me and that my actual core was bad and therefore not worthy of love. Not even my own love.

A lot of people like you and me, who are good neighbours, friends, have families, pay their taxes and bills, give to charity, help others, etc, think they are, at their core, bad. For me personally the way I saw it was that my "good behaviour" was something I did on the outside whereas if people saw my true inner self, they would see who I really was – which was bad.

And this prevented me from accepting myself, never mind loving myself. I wanted to change to become worthy of love and acceptance.

I thought that was because I sometimes had thoughts or emotions that are labelled as "bad" in our society – things like jealousy, anger, pride, irritability, hostility or resentment.

I thought to myself that if I were truly good, then I wouldn't be experiencing those things.

Because good people don't experience stuff like that, right? WRONG.

I am guessing it might sound silly because of course good people experience those things, everybody does. But you will be surprised by how many people beat themselves up for feeling/thinking negatively and let it colour their entire personality and self-worth.

Standing out

Our individuality sometimes scares us. When we hit those tween years and develop a greater sense of self and we start realizing social behaviours and the importance of being part of a group, then suddenly "fitting in" becomes important to us. We go from being free to not wanting to stand out and be different from our peers and friends. For those of us who feel like we are a little different, that can be soul destroying. Our quirks which make us special often get hidden and sometimes even forgotten and we develop the ability to "blend in", which is an important skill but, at the same time, slightly tragic.

When I say standing out I don't mean doing things that draw people's attention to you. I simply mean – being yourself. I mean resisting the urge to be like everyone else, or at least being selective about when and why we do it and have an awareness of the price we pay when we do. It could be something as small as your fashion style – I've always really loved people who have their own personal style and find it very boring how everyone seems to dress similarly, especially amongst young people. Or it could be something bigger such as how you behave, your opinions, your hobbies or the choices you make. Do you follow the herd and do certain things because everyone else is doing them, or do you follow the beat of your own heart and do your own thing?

I read somewhere that the opposite of "belonging" is "fitting in" and I can see how my desire as a human to be liked and accepted has sometimes led me to water down myself. It's natural to want to fit in, but when we feel we have to change ourselves in order to do that (and I don't mean make small adjustments in our behaviour, I mean big stuff), are we really hanging out with the right people/in the right place? Perhaps you have been told you are "too loud", "too quiet", "too bossy", "not funny", "boring", "aggressive", "too sensitive", "selfish". How did that make you feel?

Someone once told me at work that I was "intimidating" and the old me would have immediately questioned my whole essence and tried really hard to be less intimidating (whatever that means). But the years have taught me that it's not my job to worry about how other people perceive me. Let me explain – this person found me intimidating, but that didn't necessarily mean I was *being* intimidating. What one person sees as "intimidating" might be viewed as "assertive" or "driven" by another.

For women there is an added layer of judgement when it comes to our behaviour and how people see us. While men are rarely described as "bossy" or "pushy" or "too" anything, women who are confident and have opinions often are. The leap from confident to "intimidating" is very short when it comes to women, which is why these days I take less notice when people say I am "intimidating" because I know they would never say it to a man.

Finding your people

In some cases, self-reflection led me to adapt and make changes. And in some cases I came to the conclusion that I was simply with the wrong people and so instead of changing myself, I changed my surroundings. A few years ago I was invited to an industry event in London with other content creators and influencers. I had hoped to be included in this group for the longest time and I was so excited when an invitation was finally extended. At the event it became very clear to me that I didn't fit in. They simply were not my people.

Finding our people isn't something we're always taught to prioritize. That's why, when we don't fit in, we assume the problem lies with us and we go to extremes to be more acceptable. For years I forced connections that were not right for me, rather than seeking out those who truly embraced who I was. Why? Because it's not easy letting go of people or being alone. It's scary. And so many of us find it easier shrinking ourselves in order to fit in, rather than finding our people. As hard as it is, sometimes moving away from an environment that simply doesn't fit us, and embracing change, is the best approach.

And this brings me back to the idea of sisterhood and women's groups and the importance of having women in your life that support and champion you. There was a meme going around a couple of years ago that I really love; it read: "Surround yourself with women who, in a room full of opportunities, would mention your name". Those are my people. The kind of woman who holds your hair back when you've had one too many, who'll fight for you without hesitation, and who can make you laugh until your sides hurt. Women who celebrate each other's successes, who hire, mentor and promote other women, and who aren't threatened by anyone else's shine.

Ultimately, it's much easier finding yourself when you are doing it with the right people around you. In trying to be liked, to fit in, to not stand out and not ruffle feathers, we often lose sight of something important – ourselves. We bend, shrink, and compromise, trying to be everything for everyone else, and in the process forget to be true to who we are. But when we find *our people* – especially our women friends – something shifts. That acceptance gives us the confidence to stop hiding and start showing up as our authentic selves, whatever that looks like.

It's like finally exhaling after holding your breath.

I've heard multiple times from women about the cattiness and rivalry culture many of them find themselves in when it comes to their friendships with other women. But I believe that the "mean girl" culture only exists because our framework is society, and that actually if women were free of any patriarchal restraints and influence, there would be no rivalry and we'd all be braiding each other's hair around a bonfire and drinking gin and tonics.

SUGGESTION: WHO AM I?

I invite you to think again about the question "Who am I?"

Have a look at the list of words you wrote down at the beginning of this chapter and see if you feel differently about them now.

If you like, make a new list, but also remember that it doesn't have to be a list of words at all. You can write a story or a poem, you can draw an image, sing a song, put on some music and create a dance or sprinkle glitter to express yourself. Words do not need to limit you. How do you feel about what you've come up with? If you wrote down words, are there words you like? Did anything surprise you? Maybe you couldn't think of anything at all.

Remember that this is a reflection exercise – there is no right way of doing it – so please try to observe without judgement and try to have fun!

FIND YOUR POWER THROUGH FINDING YOURSELF

We're not a label or role we play in other people's lives. We're not a list of achievements, nor are we a list of qualifications, or how much money we make, how many trophies or medals we have on a shelf, how many diplomas hang on the wall, how many children or grandchildren we have, or how many years we've been married. It's not our name or how we look, and it's not even the fact we are humans who think and feel and can ponder on the question "Who am I?" to begin with. The most happy and calm people I know are the ones who allow all parts of themselves to coexist alongside each other, despite any contradictions and without judgement. There is room for everything – shame, bravery, kindness, fear, generosity, pettiness, etc. You are not one thing or another. You are an evolving story and there are many chapters yet to be discovered.

Let's "Gossip" about Megan (and a little about Ann)...

Ann is a tall woman with straight long white hair. I am not sure how old she is but I am 100 per cent sure that she has a very old soul, and I could swear that in another life she was either a wild horse or a wolf. This might sound like a random thing to say (unless you're into spirit animals), but honestly, if you met her you'd know exactly what I mean! You know people who seem to glide rather than walk? That's her, and with a twinkle in her eye she captivated me from the very first moment we met.

She is an incredible yoga teacher at a yoga studio I used to go to and her sessions are not the usual yoga I was familiar with. To be honest, it's hard to explain what she does because it's not so much *what* she does as *how* she does it. She is totally grounded yet while she teaches you how to stretch, connect and breathe, she also shares her wisdom about life and women. In short, she is amazing.

Anyway, I happened to hear a conversation she had with another woman before one of her sessions that really stuck with me. Ann was standing outside the yoga room, looking up at the stars. I had just finished my yoga class but no one was waiting to participate in the following session as it'd been added to the schedule at the last minute so clearly not many people knew about it. I was just getting my things together when Megan, another woman I'd met before at yoga, suddenly appeared.

Megan walked up to us smiling, holding her yoga mat and water bottle. I mentioned that I was on my way home and that no one else had shown up for yoga so it looked like it was just her. The news surprised her and she immediately responded with, "Oh, I see, well no, that's fine, if no one else wants to do it, I won't either. I don't want to bother you Ann, don't hold the class just for me."

Ann, ever calm, looked at Megan and with a soft and loving tone said: "Why? Are you not enough?"

Time stood still.

I was the outsider looking in as these two women stared into each other's eyes and souls, and I could tell something extraordinary was happening. Megan didn't say anything for a few moments and then she raised her head, pulled her shoulders back and said: "Yes. Yes I am."

I had witnessed a woman realizing her permission.

Permission to accept a gift, permission to take space, permission to be in the centre of her own life, permission to say, "I matter" and — above all — permission to be herself.

CHAPTER TWO
FIND YOUR POWER THROUGH GIVING YOURSELF PERMISSION

What is the first thing that comes to your mind when you think about "permission"? Take a moment to think about it. Did you immediately think about someone else who gives or denies you permission? If so, who is that? Is it a teacher? A parent? Your partner? Society? The government? God? Or is it yourself? Or perhaps you've never contemplated this? What does it feel like not to have permission, and what does it feel like when you do? What type of permission is it? Is it related to something specific in your life like food? Relationships? Sex? Something else? Or is it something bigger? The purpose of this reflection exercise is to start thinking about these ideas, be curious and ask questions. You don't have to have all the answers.

From my experience, and from many conversations I've had with the wonderful women in my life, I have realized that people have different ideas about "permission".

Some connect it to religion, while others relate it to their duties as wives/husbands/parents/employees, etc. Some have age attached to it (the saying "dress your age" limiting people's choices in terms of what they wear), status (the saying "know your place" comes to mind), etc. For a lot of people I've chatted to about permission the first thoughts that pop into their minds are related to permission they have (or don't have) *from others*. They spoke about their parents, or their partners, even society and god.

When I say permission here, though, the most important permission is from *myself* – the "yes" I give myself, not the "yes" I get from others. My own inner voice (not an outer voice), which at times was hard to hear because, like many other women, I was not taught, nor was I encouraged, to listen and follow it, as we discussed in Chapter One. This is the permission I'd like you to think about – *your own* permission, the one you were born with, no one else's.

Do you have (your own) permission? Permission to follow your heart, permission to wear whatever you want, love who you choose, study what interests you, pick your friends, take time for yourself, say "no", say "yes", set boundaries, be selfish, be silly, put yourself in the centre of your life or even at the top of your priority list, age the way you want to and follow your dreams?

In other words, do you have your permission to be yourself?

Our permission is not always easy to access, which sounds a little weird, right? Why would it be so hard for us to allow ourselves to be who we really are? Why would we not give ourselves permission to do what we want or to fulfill our own needs?

The truth is, not giving yourself permission is more common than you think. Having to fake who we are, conform, fit in, modify ourselves, adapt, please others, etc is probably something most of us do on a daily basis for various reasons – getting a job, holding a job, finding a partner, making friends, networking, etc. These are social skills we learn early in life and develop over time and they are necessary to be able to navigate the world. Of course the hope is we don't do this most of the time. In fact, I find that the natural process that happens to us – usually when we start secondary school, where we start wanting to be more like our peers and less like our individual selves because we want to be part of our equal group – is ironically something we then try to break away from as we get older.

And not all of it is bad – some social behaviours are important skills we all need to have because we live in a society with rules and codes of conduct. Some are needed for our actual survival, like learning not to play with fire or go off with strangers. And some of them have to do with acceptable social behaviour such as not putting our feet on a table in a restaurant or eating with our mouths open – even if we really want to. It is a healthy process to be able to adjust to aspects of one's society.

Not feeling permitted to be who we truly are doesn't make us happy. In the previous chapter we talked about not knowing who we are and these two things are connected. When we don't give ourselves permission to follow our heart and be who we are, it can often lead us to feel lost and disconnected. The problem is that if we've had a lot of practice in not listening to our inner voice because we've been taking our cues from others to constantly fit in and adapt, then unlearning that habit isn't easy.

For me personally it's been a process, which actually started with *recognizing* that I wasn't giving myself permission to be myself in many areas of my life.

My own permission

When I became a mother, I felt like I was thrown into the deep end with no lifejacket. I was expected to "know" how to be a mother and for things to "come naturally" on the one hand, but I was also bombarded with expert advice on how to do things "right" and I felt judged when things went wrong (which was often). People would talk about "maternal instinct", but at the same time, as women living in modern times we are somewhat disconnected from our natural instincts, and I don't think it's fair to expect it to kick into gear when you've had no practice. As a new mom I found it extremely hard to trust my own gut and follow my instincts, mainly because I didn't feel I had any. I searched for guidance everywhere and often followed what others were doing, even when it didn't feel right for me. I adopted the norms dictated by parenting books and experts to the point where I felt utterly useless – as if I couldn't trust my own judgement. It made me feel bad about myself and like I was failing, because none of it felt authentic.

I genuinely thought I wasn't a good mother because when I compared myself to other moms I felt different. Other moms loved baking and creating crafts with their kids and I honestly can't even start to tell you how much I despise doing either of those things, but I did them resentfully because I believed I was supposed to. Other moms seemed to love breastfeeding and couldn't get enough of it. I hated it and did not find it easy, yet I still tortured myself and pumped for seven months with my eldest because I couldn't allow myself to simply not do it. There were a million other big and small things that made me feel inferior and like I was blowing it daily.

At some point, when my twins were two and my eldest was four, I came to the conclusion that no one but me could do the job of being my children's mother better than I could, and that even my mistakes (of which there were many), were better for them than me feeling miserable, inauthentic and so frustrated all the time. This realization came out of sheer despair because I simply could not pretend for one more minute. It wasn't that I suddenly knew what to do or that the "maternal instinct" people spoke about finally kicked in – it was that I was willing to accept that this was what I was capable of and that it was okay, even if it wasn't perfect.

You could say that I gave myself permission to be the mother I am.

Taking charge

My version doesn't look like anyone else's because I made it up as I went along. I knew that my intentions were always good, that my aim was to be a good mother to my children, that I loved them and that I was trying my best, and that was enough. It had to be enough because it was all that I had in me. This doesn't mean I didn't ask friends for advice or research different things I wasn't sure about, but I gradually started trusting my own judgement over others when it came to my own children and I made decisions based on my (and my husband's) experience and values.

I can't even tell you how life-changing it's been. I went from feeling completely overwhelmed by all the parenting advice out there and from feeling like I was never getting it right, to feeling like I was in control, and although I didn't always get everything right, it's been a confidence-boosting experience just knowing that the kids *are* fine. I have to say, shutting out the exterior noise is brilliant. Listening inward is so much more pleasant than getting carried away by all the different exterior narratives. Especially now with the overload of information via the internet and social media, I can't even imagine how tricky it must be for new parents to navigate their way through the early days of parenting without feeling overwhelmed.

Pleasure

The same process of giving myself permission happened with food. I was about ten years old when a relative said, "You don't need that" as I reached for a second piece of chocolate after lunch. I found that comment strange; I mean, how could she know what *I* needed? After all, she wasn't me. But I also remember thinking, "Oh, maybe she is right? Maybe I don't need it and I didn't even notice? Maybe she knows my body better than I do?" This made me wonder if I could trust my own body signals. Was I really able to read them or did I need someone else to tell me when I was hungry or full. Slowly but surely the trust I had in my own ability to make choices that were best for me and my own body started being chipped away, and instead of listening to my body, I started listening to the outside world telling me what, when and how much to eat.

Nearly ten years ago, I started unpacking all of that, one step at a time, and getting back in touch with my own cravings and my body's signals. It actually started with focusing on my needs, which I talk more about later in the book, but the point is that I really had to shut all of that exterior noise out and listen inward. Some people might be familiar with the concept of "intuitive eating" – I didn't use this term, nor do I know much about it, all I know is that I got rid of the "no" and "shouldn't" when it came to food and instead replaced it with permission. Much like when you say to little children they can't have something and then that's all they want, I found that with food I had the same reaction, but when I took away the restrictions and replaced it with autonomy to choose, food lost its power over me.

After years of work, I was able to silence the outside noise and get back in touch with my own body. It wasn't about counting calories or trying to reach a goal weight like I had done throughout my teens and 20s, it was about giving myself permission to listen, trust and follow my own needs and know that I knew best.

The same goes for my career choices. I spent years pursuing a path I had no interest in just because it was the path others thought I should pursue. It took a long time to reach the point where I was able to say, "This is not for me" and give myself permission to pursue a different path for myself.

In short, the list of areas where lack of permission can show up is long and I strongly suggest you take some time to reflect on the different aspects of your own journey and see what comes up for you.

Good girls don't . . .

I want to emphasize that it might seem strange that we fail to give ourselves permission. After all, we're all adults, we should be able to do what we want and not feel any pressure to please anyone, right? But when you think about it, permission is taken away from us in different stages and places in life and often replaced with outer voices that either give their own permission, or simply take it away and give nothing in return.

I'll give you some examples: think about all the times you were told how to behave, especially as a girl. Don't be too loud, calm down, stop fussing, be a "good girl", don't sit like that/say that/pull that face. Nice girls don't swear, drink, smoke, gossip, have opinions, speak up, and so on. It's basically the speech from the *Barbie* film about the female experience, isn't it? Girls are taught not to make a fuss, not to listen to our own needs – or even have needs – but rather tend to everyone else's instead. We are taught to be nice, kind, polite, to serve others and never demand anything. Women are not encouraged to ask for raises at work or for promotions. And often if you are a woman who knows her value and isn't afraid to speak her mind and expects what she deserves, you are labelled "difficult", "bossy", "a diva", "bitchy" or "intimidating".

How can we give ourselves permission to be ourselves when the price might be being labelled a modern-day witch?

What about sex – did you ever really feel you had permission to prioritize your own pleasure? Sex and intimacy are still considered taboo topics for many, and for women in particular. Traditionally women's pleasure wasn't prioritized, and in some cases barely acknowledged. There are actually people out there who believe that the female orgasm is made up! But even without going to that extreme, women's pleasure has not been the focus. When I was younger the impression I got from movies, magazines and even conversations with other women was that sex is something women did *for men*. That the focus was *his* satisfaction and that my job was to pleasure *him*. I never stopped to think about *my* pleasure, so how could I have given myself permission to prioritize it? (I talk more about sexual pleasure and permission later in the book.)

Does any of that resonate with you?

But permission or lack of permission doesn't have to be linked to anything specific, and it doesn't have to be in the form of an obvious "no". It can be anything that makes us strive to be less ourselves and more a person who serves the needs of others around us.

So anytime you felt you had to hide a side of yourself to fit in, to be more like others and not stand out, all of those moments that you stopped yourself or when you did/said something that wasn't genuinely you because you wanted to be accepted and you knew that's what others expected from you, that all happened because you didn't have permission to be yourself.

Need to pay attention

Over time, if we are not aware, the instinctive needs, wants and desires we naturally have are slowly taken away from us, and if we do not pay attention, eventually we end up able to hear and trust our own voice less and less and we rely on other people's permission instead.

I'm sure you can identify moments in your life when other people's permission or approval of your actions – what you were wearing, how you behaved, who you were dating – felt more important than your own opinion about yourself. Maybe you wore colours that clashed and thought you looked amazing till someone told you that it didn't look good/suit you so you changed your outfit? Perhaps you didn't go on that second date because your friends didn't approve of someone even though you really enjoyed their company? Or you chose a career path to please your parents or to fit in with what others expected of you?

Small or big – most of us will have many examples.

Regaining permission is not straightforward – it's hard to break habits we've had for years. To trust ourselves and listen to our own voice when we're not used to doing that is really challenging.

It didn't happen for me in just one day; actually there were many steps to making changes (as I'll explain throughout the book) but please also know that permission from others sometimes still is important to me and that's also okay. It's natural to want to feel validated and accepted, especially by those you love and who are closest to you.

In fact, the permission I got from my online community – their support each time I said something out of the "norm box" – helped immensely. And the support of my family, particularly my husband Mike, and my friends is something that I value a lot. Sometimes the permission we get from our community and closest friends is not in the form of "yes" but rather in the form of "I am here for you". In other words, people don't have to agree with every choice you make, but if they are there for you when you need them, then that's enough.

You deserve it

I see women every day struggling to give themselves permission. With my retreats this became even clearer – so many women who desperately needed the break and reset that the retreat had to offer couldn't even bring themselves to apply, but they wrote to me privately to tell me how much they wanted to be there. They felt guilty leaving their families and giving themselves such a big gift. Even daring to think about applying made them feel like a bad person! For those who did apply, most struggled with their decision until the moment the retreat finally started. A few women signed up and then lost their nerve at the last minute and cancelled their trip – in most cases the lack of permission to do this thing that they wanted and needed for themselves was key.

That's what I want this book to give you – permission. Not from me, not from others, but from yourself: to be yourself and to prioritize your needs and your pleasure.

Permission is key to finding your power.

But HOW do you work on your permission?

FAKE IT TILL YOU MAKE IT?

A lot of people use the "fake it till you make it" tool when they are trying to make a change. What I mean is, imagine you want to become a more confident public speaker – one way to approach it is by "faking confidence". The theory is that if you pretend for long enough to be something, you will eventually either become whatever it was you were pretending to be OR people will believe that you are what you say you are – or likely both.

It's a great tool that aims to empower and encourage us to find our hidden abilities and practise them. For many people, faking it is the difference between having a job and not having one. I know plenty of introverts, for example, who have to pretend they can stomach social gatherings because it's part of their work. For some people it's the difference between having friends and not having them. It is a tool that is important and helpful, it enables many people to do things that otherwise they would not be able to do.

Personally I love the "fake it till you make it" tool and have used it for years. And you know what? It works. As someone who performs on stage from time to time, most people wouldn't know or expect that I have awful stage fright and absolutely hate it. When I tell people that, they don't believe me. "But you look so confident," they say. I fake it! The reason I do it is because I like pushing myself out of my comfort zone and I feel it is an important way to connect with my community and share my content with people and also because it's part of my work. And if I didn't have the "fake it till you make it" tool in my toolkit, I probably would never perform live, period.

Faking it allowed me to do a lot of things I don't think I could have ever done without "pretending". I defended people in court while pretending to be Ally McBeal, I performed a one-woman show in the US and the UK pretending to be Joan Rivers and I jumped out of a plane, bungee jumped and flew to the most dangerous airport in the world pretending to be a person who did not have the worst fear of heights and flights ever!

'Faking it" will look different for everyone, but for me what works is telling myself that the fear and discomfort I feel are part of the process, rather than fighting them. I have never gotten over my stage fright, but I have learnt to perform despite it. I have also chosen to believe that nerves and excitement can physically feel similar – fast heart rate, shallow breathing, and so on – and so when I feel stressed before going on stage I start saying out loud "I am so excited" instead of "I am so nervous". I don't know if this has any scientific proof but I can tell you that it works for me. It's as if I am convincing my brain that what I'm actually feeling is excitement and it helps me get on stage and do what I have to do. I can't say this has worked as well with my fear of flying – I'm still working on that one, but you find your own strategies.

From "Fake it" to "F*ck it"

But as much as I love the "fake it till you make it" tool, it has its flaws. Over time I started noticing the prices that I was paying for faking it and not being authentic *in some areas of my life*. What I mean is that while faking it allowed me to do certain things (like perform), in other areas of my life faking it didn't feel so great. Motherhood is a good example – I pretended to love messy play and baking, even though I hate baking, and don't even get me started on glitter! But I thought that baking cookies with a smile, and building crafts using a glue gun was what a "good mother" would do. That if I wanted to be a good mom (maybe even a perfect mom), I needed to do those things with my children.

Faking made me feel very resentful and angry in that situation.

I also started worrying that by not being completely honest about how I felt, I was teaching my girls to fake it too and I wasn't sure that's what I wanted for them. I didn't want them to grow up and feel like they had to be a certain type of mom or that they had to do stuff they didn't want to do just because that's what everyone else is doing.

I wanted them to know that they had freedom to choose, but obviously actions speak louder than words, so how could I convince them this was true if I wasn't doing it myself?

F*CK IT

This all happened around the time I turned 40. Lots of things happen around that age for women – hormonal changes, the kids are getting a bit older, and for many I think that's the age you feel less obligated toward society's ideas of what women need to look and behave like – and so all of that, together with how I was feeling about faking it, despite the fact it *had* worked for me for years, just brought me to the conclusion that I deserved more.

That I deserved to be myself.

Just like *you deserve to be yourself.*

And so I added a second tool to my toolkit – a little phrase that reminds me that life is too short to worry about what other people think of me, and that sometimes I just have to say "F*ck it".

How many times have you wanted to go for something but you talked yourself out of it? It can be something as small as wearing a piece of clothing you love but think people will judge you for, or as big as asking for a pay rise or a promotion. Maybe you are thinking of treating yourself to an all-girls' holiday or adventure but you don't want to be considered "selfish"? Maybe there is someone in your life that doesn't respect your boundaries and you'd like to tell them how you feel but you worry they might be offended? There are many moments in which we hear our inner voice prompting us to go for something we want or need (or both), but instead of doing it, we succumb to doubt, fear, insecurity and a sense of being undeserving of it. Sometimes the best thing you can do is think less and just go for it.

In other words, sometimes you just have to say "F*ck it".

If you watch people that take risks, they may seem fearless in that they just don't experience the same type of doubt as you. It's easy to think that others just know what to do and have bulletproof confidence. But what you might not know is that even people who take lots of risks and have confidence experience doubt. They too might question themselves and have the exact same inner dialogue you have, but they don't let it stop them. The confidence is not in the *doing of the things*, it's actually in the knowing that if they make a mistake, they've got what it takes to handle it. That they will be okay.

When I propose saying "F*ck it", I don't mean without consideration of the consequences. We care about other people's feelings and we do not set out to intentionally hurt them or disregard their needs and emotions. This is just a reminder that sometimes you have to take a leap of faith and say YES. I remind myself daily that sometimes the best things in life are beyond fear and that there is a chance the anxiety and worries I feel about different things won't go away even if I do fake it over and over again (my stage fright or fear of flying are both good examples – despite doing both things many times I still feel sick to my stomach every time I have to either go on stage or catch a flight). And so recently I have come to terms with the idea that this feeling may never go away and that I'm just going to have to say "F*ck it" and do it despite my fears.

Permission to be yourself

For some of you reading this, it may be the first time you've considered the concept of permission, and for others, you might just need that reminder. But whether this ignites a little fire or stokes an already burning flame, I want you to know that there is no right or wrong, and there is no need to compare yourself with others – your journey is unique and whatever you get out of it is perfect for you.

Keep working at it

When I did my first ever one-woman show, I decided to tell my eldest that I was scared because I wanted her to know that there will be times in her life she will be scared of doing something and I wanted her to know it's a normal feeling and that she can share it with someone close. I'll never forget what she said to me – she said: "Mommy, just be yourself." She was only eight!

Just be yourself . . . easier said than done, right? What went through my head when she said that was: but what if "myself" isn't good enough? What if people don't like me when I am myself? Our deepest fear as humans is rejection. What if we shed our armour and layers of protection and show people our true colours and they don't accept us? The older I get, the more it becomes clear that it's worth taking that risk. My strategy was to start with small things and never risk more than I was prepared to lose.

Our job on this earth is not to judge ourselves.

We have to allow ourselves to not be perfect all the time, and to look around us for support to be able to do that. And we have to have women in our life that let us be who we are. I'm thinking of that friend that you can just be yourself with, that you can show up at her doorstep and just cry, or the work colleague who shares your sense of humour and tells you when you've achieved something at work. Look for the people who see you at your lowest and don't judge, and celebrate your highs without being jealous. We need people we feel safe with to do all of it. And if you don't have those people in your life right now, that's okay – but make it a priority to start looking for the people who can be your community and circle. Seek them out.

I take it for granted now that I won't always get things right and that some people won't like me. But I would rather put it all out there and not hold back, because I know that if I do, I might miss out discovering things about myself that are worth discovering. I know that if I don't make sure I have permission to be myself, I might not find and have deeper connections with the important people in my life. And that is something I don't want to miss out on.

It takes courage to be yourself. To listen to your inner voice and let that guide you instead of someone else's voice. I think that's why many of us don't do it – it's easier to be part of the herd than to potentially stand out and be different. But when who you are on the inside is aligned with who you are on the outside, when you can hear your inner voice louder than all the other voices, when you give yourself permission to be authentic and unapologetically you, that's when you truly walk into your power.

PERMISSION TO CHANGE AND TO BE MORE YOU!

Is there something you don't give yourself permission to do/be that you are happy to play with?

My suggestion is always to start small. A good example can be clothing. Is there something you don't allow yourself to wear? It could be shorts because you don't like your legs. Maybe it's a bikini, or a dress? Can you say "F*ck it" and do it for an hour and wear whatever it is you never let yourself wear and see if you can survive the experience?

How about speaking up the next time that you're discussing going out or doing something with friends or family – instead of doing whatever you know will make others happy, think about what you want to do.

Identify the decisions you make every day that you can give yourself permission to do honestly and authentically. Find something relatively small and see if you can give yourself permission to do it for an hour and see how that

FIND YOUR POWER THROUGH GIVING YOURSELF PERMISSION

feels. Remember that unlearning something that's so deeply ingrained in us (listening to other people's opinions rather than your own) is not easy and takes time, so be gentle with yourself.

What we want is to start practising giving ourselves permission to be who we are and to follow our own inner voice, so start with things that feel easier and work your way up. If you think you can tackle bigger areas then go for it!

Let's "gossip" about Clara and Sharon...

I work with Sharon and she is always in charge of the schedules, which suits her perfectly as she is the type of person that gets very excited about a colour-coordinated Excel spreadsheet (and I say this as a compliment because her organizational skills are truly phenomenal). Her ability to run a tight ship allows me to focus on the content knowing that someone was making sure things were ticking along according to plan.

On the second evening of the retreat we had a Shamanic ceremony planned with Clara, who I had worked with before and absolutely adore. I met her in Lisbon when I attended a women's circle and we instantly clicked. Her out-of-this-world vibe really drew me to her: she has this calm energy that immediately puts me at ease and I find myself smiling for no reason when I am in her presence.

Clara doesn't have a watch and time is just a loose idea to her, so when she texted to say she was running late, I wasn't surprised. A while later I got a panicked text message from Sharon telling me that Clara had finally arrived but was now insisting on having dinner before starting her session. I giggled to myself at the interaction between these two women who were complete opposites.

I told everyone that the ceremony would start a little later than planned and headed over to the kitchen where I found Clara eating her dinner slowly and with immense pleasure, and Sharon sitting beside her sweating and fuming with rage. After she finished her dinner she guided us through the Shamanic ceremony, which was divine and all was well.

Later that night when I got a chance to chat to Sharon, she was able to vent about how annoyed she had got with Clara's slowness and the fact she "had the nerve" to eat dinner before conducting her session when she was already late. She told me that when Clara arrived she told her that she needed to rush because she was behind schedule, but Clara very calmly said, "I need to eat first." She didn't apologize or make any excuses, she just said what she needed and trusted that this was enough.

The next day Clara was doing yoga and some breathing exercises and she invited Sharon to join her. I don't think Sharon has time for breathing in her usual busy schedule but for whatever reason she said yes and she joined in. Clara likes sharing insights and wisdom when she teaches, so throughout this impromptu session she spoke about time and patience —and above all, listening to our needs.

When Sharon returned from her session with Clara she was a changed person.

She was so grateful to have had the opportunity to get a new perspective from Clara and had also realized something profound about herself. In her attempt to be "perfect" — the perfect mother, wife, friend, person with Excel spreadsheet in charge of the schedule, etc — she completely ignored her own needs. Everyone else's needs were what she paid attention to and tried to address, while her own were totally forgotten about.

When Clara said "I need to eat first" it triggered Sharon to the core because she couldn't comprehend how this woman had the audacity to put her own needs ahead of other people. Sharon deemed her selfish, unprofessional and even rude, just for acknowledging and addressing her needs, and when she saw this she realized how disconnected she had become from her own needs.

It was a life-changing experience for Sharon, one that would start a new journey for her getting to know her needs away from her Excel spreadsheets.

CHAPTER THREE
FIND YOUR POWER THROUGH ADDRESSING YOUR NEEDS

How often do you ask yourself what you need? Are you aware of your needs? How does it make you feel when you think about attending to your needs? Do you give yourself permission to prioritize them, or is thinking about your needs something you rarely do? Please close your eyes for a moment and really think about these questions. Ask yourself, "What do I need?" Have you ever asked this before? Has anyone else ever asked you? How does it feel to be asked? Do you have an answer or is it so foreign that you can't even think of anything?

Dr Tilly Paz introduced me to this question, which honestly changed my life, and I am hoping it does the same for you. A few years ago I was working with her during a period in my life I now refer to as my "awakening" because I awakened to the idea that I have *never* thought about my needs, and it was the first step I took towards being a more real version of myself. I consider her to this day my greatest teacher. Her commitment to being herself inspired and challenged me in equal measures and ultimately pushed me to find my own authenticity, and for that I will always be grateful. I still remember the day she asked me for the first time, "Tova, what do you need?"

This question is part of giving yourself permission to be yourself, female empowerment and being able to answer the illusive question "Who am I?" I believe that giving ourselves permission to be ourselves can only happen *when we know and listen to our needs*. And it's not an easy thing to identify our needs – some are linked to our values and core beliefs, and are tough to unpack. But we're also going to talk about needs as simple things – some fresh air and time by ourselves, a nourishing meal or steaming bath, or even a hug when we need physical comfort.

The toughest question

When I realized in my early 40s that I had lost sense of who I was, apart from being someone's mother and wife, it made me feel very disconnected from myself. Motherhood, breastfeeding, how my body had changed, all meant that I didn't feel like my own body even belonged to me. It was a massive identity crisis and I felt like a stranger to myself on so many levels (who is this angry woman constantly shouting at her kids?).

One of the biggest aids to help me reconnect with myself was getting to know my *needs*. Why? Because my needs pointed me in the right direction. They focused me and put me at the centre of my life.

For many people, especially women, putting ourselves in the centre of their own life feels threatening. It makes us feel selfish. It is an unacceptable idea for many, and at times it seems like we need permission just to imagine it. This is especially true for the many women who are the primary caregivers of their families or carers with a responsibility to serve and self-sacrifice, often at the expense of our own needs.

When I first asked myself "What do I need?" I started to cry because for the first time I became aware of the fact that I hadn't asked myself that question . . . ever. And if I did, then I couldn't remember when. What I knew for sure was that I hadn't asked it in a long time and I had no idea how to even start answering it.

I was faking being satisfied in many areas of my life.

Women are often encouraged to be "grateful" for things and if we question what we have, we are labelled as "difficult" or "ungrateful". Is it just me, or does anyone else feel like chucking their gratitude journal out of the window sometimes? Don't get me wrong, I'm all for finding the silver lining and appreciating what we have – that's the whole point of gratitude, right? But have you ever noticed how this seems to be something pushed on women more than men? It's of course a positive thing to be able to see the good in anything and that's what being grateful is all about – focusing on what you have as opposed to what you don't have. But it should never come at the cost of ignoring what's not working or feeling like we can't voice when we want or need more.

If you're a mother who admits she finds motherhood hard, people are quick to point out that some women can't have children. I clearly remember feeling like I couldn't say I was struggling or that I needed help because people around me kept saying how lucky I was to be a mother and so I should just get on with it and be grateful. I was faking enjoyment of motherhood and never asked what I still needed, as a woman, regardless of being a mom. Faking happiness with my body, not asking what I needed to actually love it. Faking satisfaction with my sex life without exploring my need for pleasure.

Being clear

Needing something is different to wanting something, although sometimes what we need and what we want can be the same thing. I knew this, but for years I had been programmed to focus on "wants" rather than needs. In fact, our society teaches us to shut out our needs, and focus on our wants instead. We are asked from an early age what we want, but very rarely what we need, so we simply don't get enough practice in thinking about it. "What do you want to eat?"

rather than "What does your body need to feel nourished?" "What job do you want?" rather than "What do you need from your job?" "What type of partner do you want?" rather than "What type of qualities do you need in your partner in order to feel secure/loved, etc?" If you play with the above questions you might find that the answers you give to what you want vs what you need are different.

It's rare that people are asked what they need, but we are often asked what we want.

As a result of this we think that our wants are our needs and we also think that if we get what we want, it will make us happy – but in reality we often find that when we get what we want, we are still not happy.

What we *want* is often material stuff – a bigger house, more money or nice clothes; or a feeling or a state of mind – we want to be happy, healthy, calm, etc. And it can also be superficial – I want an attractive partner, for example, which doesn't address why certain things are important to us. But when we focus on our needs we go deeper and this often leads us to uncover much more profound insights about ourselves.

For example, when I would say, "I want something sweet" I would not really question this desire. But when I changed it to "I need something sweet" it was easier to then say, "I need something sweet right now because I am feeling down and I need something to cheer me up." This then led me to make the connection between eating sweet/comforting food when I felt down, which then led me to tackle the real issue – why I was feeling down, which eventually led me to see what I *really* needed, and it rarely was something sweet.

But what are "needs" and what is the difference between our needs and our wants?

A need is defined as "essential . . . rather than merely desirable".[18] But we are going to use a wider definition of needs because I'm not just talking about oxygen, food and water.

You can want a bigger house, but you don't *need* it to live a happy and healthy life. You can want nice clothes, a fat bank account, a Chanel bag and a pair of Jimmy Choos, but you don't *need* any of them to have a stable and happy life.

Jane Connor, PhD and Dian Killian, PhD wrote "needs are the driving energies of life" and I like that definition because I see our needs as our guides through life, because not only do they push us to take action, but they enable and encourage us to take the *right* action.[19]

In other words – if we listened to our needs we would take actions in our life in a way that would make us feel good. Needs, when left unfulfilled, can result in lack of energy and engagement, irritability, inability to focus and sadness, which is exactly how I felt when I started my own journey.

The twofold challenge is to identify those needs, and then to listen to them.

For me it was *really* hard and I actually don't think I even knew that I had needs in the first place, let alone that they were unmet. When your needs are not met, a void is created and we often try to fill the void with something else. Some people use alcohol or drugs, for me it was food. I would eat to block out the pain, and to avoid asking myself that simple question – *what do I need?* Not addressing need can be the core of addiction. It's as though we fill the pain created by not listening to our needs with something that will distract us further from what we actually require. It takes us away from sitting in the discomfort of not having our needs met. We scroll on the phone, eat, drink alcohol, take drugs or smoke in order to temporarily make us feel better, and we might forget for a while. But no matter how much we try, we will never feel satisfied because we haven't addressed the actual needs that are not being met.

So I started asking myself this question every time I found myself walking up to my fridge in the evenings and opening the door to take out whatever it was – I would pause for one second and ask myself what did I need? Because I knew the answer was not really chocolate.

It was a long process – it didn't take just one day. I would ask that question and not really know how to answer it, but eventually answers started coming to me, and the truth is – they were very painful.

At that time I was unhappy with my marriage and I was very unhappy with my body. I felt like I had lost touch with my own sexuality, so there were a lot of things going on, and the answers I started getting to that question were things like: I need a hug, I need to be touched, I need sex, I need passion, I need to feel young again . . . all of which were hard to admit.

For me it was a combination of physical and emotional needs that I had just completely ignored for so long, and becoming aware of this was a powerful process, but also difficult.

Why needs are so hard to recognize

Those needs essential to our very survival – like food, air, water and sleep – are obvious and sometimes they are still not met. The need for rest is a classic one and I am sure there are many women out there who can relate to this. We all know rest and sleep are important, yet many of us find ourselves up far too late aimlessly scrolling on TikTok, not getting enough sleep and then finding ourselves tired the next morning. The same can be said about food – we all know what foods are nourishing yet we don't always eat them. Some days we fuel our bodies with nothing but crap despite knowing this is not what our bodies need. We might also smoke and drink alcohol which we know our bodies *don't* need at all. What I am trying to say is that even our basic physical needs are sometimes ignored – that's how trained we are to not listen to our needs even when they are super easy to spot and identify.

So imagine how much harder it is to fulfill other needs, like your emotional or spiritual or creative needs, those that are not strictly necessary for your survival!

Several factors can make it difficult for us to recognize or acknowledge our needs. For one, not recognizing our needs means we don't have to be in a painful place. But beyond that, when it comes to recognizing emotional needs in particular, I would say that we're not really taught to do that. It's linked to other ideas I've already talked about – not being taught to listen to our inner voice but rather always look outward. The same can be said about our needs. We're not really brought up to trust our own body's signals about even the most basic thing like hunger, so how can we ever be expected to trust our body's signals about the emotional stuff?

> ## SUGGESTION: IDENTIFYING YOUR NEEDS
>
> Take a piece of paper and draw a big question mark. Feel free to decorate it, or leave it as it is. Stick it somewhere you will see it often throughout the day like on the fridge door, or on a mirror or the wall in your bedroom. I want it to be somewhere you will see it often and use it as a frequent reminder to ask yourself "What do I need right now?"
>
> Then take some time to make a list of your needs – don't feel that this has to be a complete list, just start with something – touch, security, love, sex, movement, laughter, excitement, freedom, good food, sisterhood ... whatever comes to mind. Can you give yourself permission to believe that your needs, some of the time, should and could be in the centre of your life? What does it feel like? How long can you keep holding the thought? If this is easy for you – fantastic! Next, you can ask yourself when it is that you stop putting your needs in the centre? Who or what makes it easier or harder?
>
> Your needs are often easy to satisfy, they just need your attention. For example, think about your biggest physical need. We will take movement as a good example to work with. On a scale of 1 to 10, how much do you need movement in your life?

We now want to define what would satisfy you for each step of the scale, up to the level you want to have in your life. To start with, can you think what would satisfy you for level 1? It could be stopping what you do for one minute, and moving your hips. It could be waving your arms like a mad woman. It could be shaking your head or running in place for 30 seconds. It could also be just stopping for a few deep breaths. Try it with me? I like doing neck rolls . . . feels so good! Is there satisfaction in that for you? Does it feel good to attend to this need?

If there is, what will give you a satisfaction level of two? Work your way up until you complete the scale to the level you want to have in your life? Find what things bring you to that level.

SUGGESTION: FOCUS TO START UNDERSTANDING YOUR NEEDS

To practise focusing on needs rather than wants, write down on a piece of paper some of your wants – anything from career to dating or the type of holidays you want to go on. Examples can include: I want a sports car, I want a bigger house, I want to get married, I want to have my own brand, I want to fit into my size 12 dress again, I want to get a degree, I want children, I want chocolate, I want to have more friends . . .

Once you've made your list, choose one of the items and focus on it. Ask yourself if this "want" also represents a need, and if so, what is that need? For example, let's say you choose to focus on "I want to fit into my size 12 dress again." Ask yourself in relation to this specific item what it is that you need? Chances are you don't *need* to fit into your size 12 dress but maybe what you need is to feel attractive or desired? Keep asking "What do I need?" and see if you can peel off the layers to find out what is at the heart of the want.

In this example you might discover a need for acceptance or self-worth – maybe you associate being a size 12 with feeling valued, admired or loved by others? You might discover a need for self-confidence because you might believe that achieving a certain size will boost your confidence. This might lead you to realize that what you truly need is to work on your self-esteem and appreciate your body in its current state. You might discover that it comes from a need for control – especially if other parts of your life feel unpredictable or overwhelming.

Another example might be "I want a new job". If you pause and focus on your needs it will help you not only to understand why you want a new job, but also what you need this new job to have so that it is right for you. Possible deeper needs might include fulfilment, respect or balance. You might be seeking to feel appreciated, challenged, or to escape burnout in your current position.

The point is that reflecting on needs vs wants sets you in the right direction so that you can address the underlying need directly, rather than rely on the surface-level want to fulfill it.

Befriend your needs

We often carry this belief that having needs makes us "needy", and that being needy somehow makes us pathetic or weak. It's almost as if admitting we need something is seen as a flaw. I think a lot of this comes from how many of us were raised with the idea that showing vulnerability is a sign of weakness. But I hope anyone reading this knows that couldn't be further from the truth. There's so much strength in being able to ask for something, and there's absolutely no shame in having needs. Everyone does! How powerful is a woman who knows what she needs and takes steps to meet those needs? A woman who shows up for herself, unapologetically? That's not weakness – that's strength. That's self-respect. A woman like that doesn't just survive – she thrives.

I know that for some of you this might sound like a very big task, but as with any other journey, you can start by making very small steps. Moving my body was the first need I addressed when I was struggling to identify what I needed. It was more about finding something that I genuinely liked doing that also involved moving my body rather than "exercising", and for me that was dancing. I joined a pole dancing class with women who were mostly half my age, and at first, I'll admit, I felt intimidated. But the connection we share as women made all the difference. They were supportive, welcoming, and any apprehension I had quickly faded. Dancing alongside them became not just a fun activity that addressed my need for movement and to regain my sexuality, but it was also an incredibly empowering and liberating experience. It reminded me of the strength we find in one another, and how that shared encouragement helps to create a space where we can be celebrated, and free to express ourselves.

It didn't have to be pole dancing; the point was addressing my need for movement and if you have the same need then find something that suits you. Moving our bodies makes us feel good, especially if we move it in a way that's fun, when we don't feel like it's a punishment. It can be anything – walking, dancing, maybe you like yoga or stretching, whatever brings you pleasure.

Female rage

I have this gag I tell at my shows which always gets a big laugh: I say that as the years have gone by I've felt this thing bubbling inside me and that it's gotten bigger and bigger. And then, in my 40s I finally realized that the ring women get across the middle of their bodies isn't a ring of fat, like the experts say it is. It is actually a ring of anger and resentment.

They say there is truth in every joke and this is something I do think is true. Women are angry, and with good reason. The gender pay gap globally is about 20 per cent; one in three women worldwide have experienced physical or sexual violence by a partner or sexual violence from a non-partner; 12 million girls under 18 are married each year; women hold just 26.5 per cent of parliamentary seats across the world. And in countries such as Afghanistan and the US, girls currently have fewer rights than their mothers and grandmothers.[20]

But on top of all of that, women are also angry because prioritizing our needs and setting boundaries don't come naturally to us, and when we put ourselves first, we are accused of being selfish and vilified. Is it really so surprising that so many women experience "female rage"?

The other day I had a crazy deadline at work and my kids just kept expecting me to tend to their needs even though I told them I needed to work. I closed the office door and asked to be left alone to work, yet one by one they came in with their requests. My frustration was worse as I know that when Mike is working no one disturbs him and he has the privilege of uninterrupted hours in the office. At some point I snapped and screamed in rage that everyone should leave me alone. Women's rage is bottled – we don't express our needs/frustrations because we don't feel we can look after ourselves/take time for ourselves, and our needs eventually overwhelm us and we explode.

> ## SUGGESTION: STARTING SMALL
>
> If you're struggling to know where to start, then try these prompts:
> - Pause and ask: "What do I need?" "What am I really looking for?"
> - Focus on feelings: Try to identify the emotions connected to the want (this will help you shift it from wants to needs) – love, acceptance, excitement, security, etc.
>
> As always my suggestion is to start small.
>
> What would happen if you addressed your physical need for creativity or getting out into nature once a week? Can you do it more? How do you feel after you do it? What about your need for "me time" – can you dedicate an hour a week just for you? What about your need to have more time with your female friends – can you commit to a weekly get-together with your girlfriends?
>
> When approaching the idea of satisfying our needs, start with micro-needs and micro-satisfaction. It means that you find the smallest unit of the need, and the smallest unit of satisfaction, and you give yourself permission just for that, to start with. The beauty of the micro approach is that it doesn't take time, and is easy to approach, even if you are struggling with the general concept of attending to your needs. Instead of focusing on the big stuff, start small – it's about setting things in motion, starting the conversation and getting into a new habit.

A major need I recognized was the need to connect with other women. I didn't know this was a "need" until I had it back in my life. Sisterhood, being with women and honouring women, laughter and celebration with women is a need most of us have but we don't prioritize. It is the need of community, or being with people who understand what we are going through, who champion us and who allow us to show up as we are. I can't tell you how important addressing this need is in your journey to finding your power, and I will talk more about this in later chapters.

When I started my own work on what was missing from my life, one of the hardest things was actually dedicating the time to myself. Even going out for a daily walk in the woods felt like a lot to ask. The sink was full of dishes, the laundry needed doing, I had work to do. How could I possibly go out for a walk, let alone a long walk in the woods listening to music and soaking in the fresh air? But when you're trying to focus on yourself, I find it helpful to think of the importance of showing that I respond to my own needs. When I rest, I show my daughters that they can too. When I say no to an obligation, I show others that I have needs too, and remind them that I am my own person and need to be cared for also – by myself and by those around me. In the end the time I gave myself is what opened up many things for me. I suddenly had new ideas, I felt better physically, healthier and generally my mood was better.

What I am trying to say is that I had to prioritize *myself* and *my needs* and I think that's the hardest thing to do – but it is so worth it.

LET'S TALK ABOUT
LETTING GO OF SHAME

What comes to mind when you think about shame? Are there things in your life you feel ashamed of? Have they impacted your relationships with others? What even does the word mean to you? Shame is one of those unspoken emotions that does a lot of damage to people when it is allowed to sit unchallenged and buried. Start by writing down a few words that come to mind when you consider your relationship with shame.

Guilt and shame are obstacles that we're going to need to talk about if we're intending to prioritize our wants and needs, and who we are. These two baddies are often confused, but they're essentially ways that we judge and criticize ourselves, and that can hold us back from moving forward and from feeling deserving of good things.

Shame is something many struggle with but its power stems from the assumption that it is just us who feel it, that it relates to something no one else has done/would do. There was a time when I wasn't sure about the difference between shame and guilt – I might have thought they were both the same thing, so let's just clear this up.

I like to think of guilt as something we feel about an action we've done or not done. For example, when I once forgot my daughter's birthday assembly at school I felt immense mom guilt. I didn't think I was a bad person, I just felt really bad about my actions. It's also when I snap at the kids or my husband because I've had a hard day, or if I haven't spent enough time with the children, or if I've eaten a whole tub of ice cream (actually I never feel guilty about doing that). The point is, guilt often feels contained within the premise of whatever event it is related to and doesn't make me question myself as a whole. Guilt is that little nudge in the back of your brain that tells you, "Hey, I messed up here." It can be very helpful because it makes you want to reach out, apologize, make things right, and maybe even not make the same mistake again. In a way, guilt can be motivating and bring about a positive outcome, because it encourages us to be better next time.

What is shame?

Shame, on the other hand, is very different. It can be about an event or events, or something done by you, or done to you, but the difference is that it makes you think of yourself in a negative light. When I feel shame I question if I am good, if I am worthy of love, if I deserve to be happy. Instead of thinking, "I did something bad," shame says, "I *am* bad." It takes over how you see yourself as a person. When we feel shame, it's like we're convinced there's something essentially wrong with *who we are* – not just what we did. And instead of wanting to fix the situation, shame often makes you want to hide away and shut down.

You've probably heard of Brené Brown, a leading researcher on shame and vulnerability. She argues that "shame thrives in secrecy, silence, and judgement" and if you haven't read any of her books or watched her Ted Talks, I strongly suggest you look them up.[21] I've found so much truth in her thoughts about how shame thrives in darkness. From my own life I know that when I've had this heavy emotion, I've kept it to myself, because the thought of sharing it with anyone was far too scary. Shame makes you believe you are bad – imagine how petrifying it is to share that with others? What if they think you're bad too? What if they hate you? What if they are disgusted by you? Or worse – leave you?

It is natural to want to hide shame and what I also noticed is that the secrecy made my feelings of shame even worse as time went by. The darkness was like a fertilizer for shame and the longer and harder I tried to keep it hidden, the bigger it got.

Does any of that sound familiar?

Everyone experiences shame. When we carry this heavy load it can often feel like it's just us, especially when we're not talking about it with anyone. We look around us and think that this thing that's wrong with us is something no one else would understand, because no one else can be as awful as we are. But actually shame is universal and it's often linked to taboo topics people don't like or feel able to talk about, even though a lot of people experience them.

In short, it's not just you.

Toxic shame

Obviously there are different levels of shame and at the far end, when it's really toxic, often comes a sense of worthlessness. Toxic shame often takes root during childhood or early adolescence, when we're still figuring out who we are and forming our sense of self-worth. It's usually tied to trauma such as abuse, neglect, or an experience that deeply wounds us emotionally.[22] When something traumatic happens, especially when it involves people we trust, it's easy to internalize their hurtful actions or words. Instead of recognizing the unfairness of the situation, we might start to believe that *we're* the problem, absorbing feelings of worthlessness that don't actually belong to us.

It's important to note that toxic shame doesn't necessarily mean you're feeling ashamed all the time – it doesn't have to be constantly present 24/7, but it can linger, shaping how we see ourselves and impacting our relationships and decisions long into adulthood. It can impact our sex lives, relationships, how we parent, how we see our bodies and more, and nearly every woman I have ever met carries some shame with her.

We need to talk more about shame

Shame loses its power when we shine a light on it.

From my own experience I can tell you that only when I dared to share my shame with others did I see how taking it out of the shadows into the light helped start to dissolve it. When you say something aloud and you realize that the world hasn't ended, it gives you your power back.

The other important part of all of this is, of course, empathy – another topic Brené Brown talks about. The idea of your shame being met with empathy rather than judgement, something we were able to create at the retreats with the women circles, is life-changing. Being able to say out loud things that we feel shameful about is by itself healing, but imagine how much more powerful that is when it's met with empathy and even love.

A tool against women

Shame is a wonderful way to oppress women.[23] I know so many women who dare not talk about their sexual fantasies because society tells women that sexual pleasure is shameful. I know women who dare not talk about how they sometimes hate being mothers because society tells them that mothers who feel that way should be ashamed of themselves. Even the stereotype of the "gossiping women" paints a picture of women as lazy and focused only on trivial, malicious chatter.

It's a way to shame women into thinking that our voices and conversations don't matter.

But they do.

The point is that, in the quest to find your female power, stepping out of the darkness away from shame and into the light is a major step in the right direction.

> ## ACKNOWLEDGEMENT AND SHARING
>
> At the retreats we divided into smaller groups and encouraged everyone to share their shame. The idea was to just say one or two sentences and then move to the next person. One person at a time would speak as the others listened and said nothing. We reminded everyone that in order to create a safe space that allowed people to share their shame with confidence, no one was to judge or offer advice, but everyone was invited to show love and empathy. I took part in several of these sessions and I am always amazed by how painful, powerful and empowering this exercise is. The women shared many stories and their shame touched on the way they felt about their bodies, their relationships with their parents, sex, trauma and more. It brought up a lot of emotions and we had a team of facilitators supporting those who needed support, but overall the takeaway was the same – shame shrinks when you shine a light on it.
>
> There isn't a way for me to practise this specific exercise through a book so, I suggest getting curious about your shame if you can.
>
> Acknowledging it is the first step. We cannot work on something we are not aware of. Ask yourself if you feel shame? If the answer is yes (likely because most people experience shame), ask yourself what sort of impact it has

on your life? Does it stop you from forming connections with people? Does it impact your sex life? Does it make you see yourself in a really bad light? Shame is experienced in different ways and on different levels, and if what you feel is a deep sense of worthlessness, depression or anxiety, then you might want to reach out to a professional who can help you work through it.

Start to note what things, or people, trigger feelings of shame for you, as setting clear boundaries could help reduce the fraction and reduce these situations.

Please be kind and compassionate with yourself – we are fast to judge ourselves.

Finally, getting support is key – whether it's from a professional, a support group, your friends, family or someone else you trust who can lend an ear, be supportive and offer empathy. Sharing how you feel can help in taking away shame's power over you.

Let's "gossip" about Isabella...

Isabella worked in finance for years. She was senior in her company, made lots of money, had the house, the car, two beautiful kids and a husband that idolized her. Her life seemed perfect. She didn't mind the long hours or the business trips and her plan was to work hard, save money and then retire early(ish), though her husband never believed she would ever opt for a calmer type of life because she loved the adrenaline too much.

Three years ago she got breast cancer.

After an aggressive course of treatment, which also resulted in a full mastectomy and a painful recovery, once she was finally cancer free and got the all clear from her doctors, Isabella quit her job, packed her bags and moved the entire family to Greece.

When I spoke to her a year after they had made the big move, she said it was the best decision they had ever made. Her husband works remotely online but they have opted for a simpler life and didn't stress over money as much as they had. She had taken up pottery, cooking, snorkelling and other fun activities she used to do when she was young but never got round to doing later as life got in the way.

We have spoken several times about the "meaning of life" since her diagnosis, as I am always fascinated by people's perspectives, especially if they have had a near-death experience or have overcome an illness.

"Playing," she replies, "having fun and playing, that's what it's all about."

CHAPTER FOUR
FIND YOUR POWER THROUGH PLAYFULNESS

I could have named this chapter "Find Your Power Through Joy". I didn't use it because I think the word joy can sometimes intimidate people. It's a high-level word. It's more than just being happy. It feels like something almost achievable for many people because it is associated with a state of mind, something we can maybe aim for after all the other things fall in line. It can also come across as an end goal – a destination we want to get to rather than something that we can incorporate in our day-to-day life. And all of that can put people off. That's why I chose the word "playfulness" instead. It feels more inviting, a little less scary and more realistic. You don't have to be happy or full of joy; you just need to find moments of playfulness in your life. Feels more doable, right?

Do you have playfulness in your life? Think about that question for a moment. How much of your day or week is dedicated to simple fun and joy compared to how much of it is dedicated to getting through your "to-do list", working and sorting the logistics of life – what to eat, washing clothes and so on? What could be stopping you from making more time to "play"? Can you even picture what that looks like? Maybe the idea of playing feels silly when you are an adult with responsibilities. Do you believe playing is just for children and, if so, when did you start believing that? Write down anything that pops to mind right now and just sit with it for a while.

When we are driven to work hard, when we are trying our best to be perfect, when we are constantly focused on achieving our goals and looking after everyone around us, we forget our playfulness. Remember that childlike joy of simply having fun? It's a lost art for many adults who are desperately trying to find validation through achievements, appearances, finances and other labels, so much so that in the process we sacrifice one of the best features of life.

Joy.

I would argue that playing is the key to joy. You see, when we play like children, we put aside our analytic brains, we stop overthinking and judging ourselves, we no longer focus on achievements and to-do lists, and instead we allow our inner child to come through. We make room for our creativity, we connect with other people on a totally different level and, most importantly, we are present in the moment.

Endorphin rush

Also – playing makes us feel good – I mean, playing is fun! Remember fun? When did we stop having it?

Scientists will even tell you why having fun makes us feel so good in the moment, and has lots of physical and mental benefits. It's connected to the release of endorphins, the chemicals in our brains that promote feelings of pleasure and well-being. Engaging in playful activities, especially anything that also involves laughter, movement and being outdoors, stimulates the brain to release these happiness hormones, which in turn affects and reduces stress (by lowering our cortisol). Playing can even improve our cognitive function – the happy hormones facilitate improved memory and learning capacity, and help with focus. We've all noted the effects when we learn or have experiences with a fun teacher or while having a good time with friends – the brain seems more receptive and open to being creative, problem-solving or processing information.[24]

In short, having fun is good for us!

Plus, all work and no play makes for a pretty miserable existence.

Growing up

Peter Pan's advice was never to grow up, and I think this is one of the best tips out there. It's okay to take on the responsibilities of life and looking after ourselves, and others in our care, but why does this mean we completely let go of that part of us that is playful, childlike, naive, curious, enthusiastic and inquisitive?

Ironically we spend our early years longing to grow up. It's natural to want more freedom, more independence and even more responsibilities. But when did getting older mean turning our backs on our inner child? When do we lose the freedom we are born with – to be daring, and to not care so much about making mistakes or what other people think of us? When do we grow out of just having fun for no particular reason, and what can we do about that?

If you look at kids when they play, especially younger children, you see how few inhibitions they have. No idea is too silly, and they don't judge themselves for their ideas. There is no need for planning or long negotiations; they just jump in and get going.

"Imagine this is a fort and I am a princess and you are a prince and we have to kill the dragon!"

"Yes! And imagine I have a horse and his name is Stanley and he can fly when he hears music!"

"Yes! And imagine I can speak dragon so in the end we don't have to kill the dragon because it becomes our friend!"

"Yes!" And so on . . .

The world of children is a world of imagination and endless possibilities! But there is a point in every child's life that they are told to grow up.

Winnie-the-Pooh's friend, Christopher Robin, had to grow up and leave the Hundred Acre Wood because it was time for him to go to school. This is what all children are expected to do at some point – to put down the toys and get serious – because life is serious and we are told that we can't spend our lives playing. We transition from children into preteens and teenagers and eventually young adults. We are expected, and in some cases even encouraged, to put stuffed toys in a drawer and replace them with books, calculators and make-up kits. Playgrounds become the place where younger children play, and while they might want to join in, teens see themselves as too old for that now.

In today's world this process seems to be happening earlier. Children's access to social media and the internet makes them grow up faster than ever before and the increasing pressure from the schooling systems has also meant that the "rat race" most of us resent and wish we could get out of is imposed on young children at an even younger age than it was on us.

There are people out there who believe that secondary school students are too old for fun stuff and that they should solely focus on academics. Schools start conversations about careers with kids as young as 11. The rationale being that it's a competitive world and they better get onto the competitive ladder or they risk being left behind. Add to that the mature content many are exposed to online and the result is that our kids are being told directly and indirectly that they need to grow up before they even hit puberty.[25]

I think it's awful.

Let kids be kids is what I think. Rather than accept that they are growing up way too fast and hop on the train, try to delay the process as much as possible. As parents we can't control everything, but collectively, together with schools, we have more power than we think and we should at least try. I tell my kids every day that their job is to play. It's one of the many little things I do to try and balance the speeding train their generation seems to be on, growing up far earlier than they should.

Staying young (at heart)

Growing up is of course a natural part of life, but letting go of our inner child need not be. This is particularly challenging though for women, especially when we transition into motherhood. Being someone's parent changes our perspective, and the overwhelming responsibility of caring, nurturing and raising another human being often comes at the expense of our own sense of adventure and the light-heartedness that is associated with being young, selfish and more childlike. We feel we must grow up for the sake of our children who need a parent – a grown-up – to guide them, to teach them right from wrong and protect them.

I felt a massive shift in me when I became a mother. I went from being someone who enjoyed travelling and a certain amount of risk (I used to snowboard in my 20s and I even skydived in my 30s before having children) to someone who felt like I had too much to lose if anything happened to me. In fact, I felt guilty even considering anything risky *because* I was a mother. I had a job to do, a commitment toward my kids and so any element of adventure and risk taking was out of the question.

Society enforces this idea in women. The media reports on "mothers" who died in accidents while climbing a mountain or taking part in some extreme sport – but never "fathers". Women's responsibilities as mothers are put under a microscope, we are held to the highest expectations – to be careful, safe, serious, responsible and 100 per cent dedicated to serving our children's needs, but never our own. So much so that a term was invented for what many mothers feel whenever they do anything that isn't selfless – our "mom guilt".

A few years ago I travelled to Nepal with my brother for nearly three weeks and the "mom guilt" was terrible. I felt as if I had abandoned my children, even though they were left behind with their father who took excellent care of them in my absence. It was an irrational reaction that almost led me to cancel the whole trip, but my husband insisted I go, reminding me that he is very capable of taking care of his own children, which he most certainly is.

Apart from saying goodbye to my sense of adventure, becoming a parent meant that I also said goodbye to a part of me that was more childlike, the part of me that didn't worry so much and was always ready to say "yes". The part that didn't overthink or catastrophize. The part that didn't have everything figured out and planned months in advance. The part that was free and relaxed and present.

Without realizing, becoming a mother to my own children finalized the process of saying goodbye to my own inner child, fully growing up and becoming a boring adult.

But what if I told you that growing older doesn't mean having to let go of your inner child? What if we could hold on to that part of us that ran barefoot on the beach with nothing but a diaper on and chocolate ice cream covering our face, living our best life? What if we can laugh out loud and be silly at any age and never let go of the joyful spark we had when we were little? What if adventures are not just for the young? What if life is all about taking risks and not playing it too safe? What if we can be responsible adults that pay their taxes, go to work and make sure our kids are looked after – *and also* play?!

I don't mean play all day or ignore the commitments you have – that would be irresponsible of me to suggest. We all have people who rely on us – we can't just not do things. But I also know that one choice doesn't have to cancel out the other. I find that using "and also" here really works. I know that having a holistic view of ourselves rather than a binary view ("I am this *or* that") means that anything we want to be true about ourselves and our lives *can be*.

So how do we introduce (or indeed invite back) playfulness into our lives?

This always feels like such a massive task for people when you first bring it up. So many women at my retreat say on the first day how they haven't laughed in years and by the end of day two they can barely control their laughter. This is very often one of the biggest takeaways from the retreats, and what you might not believe is that it didn't take much for that to happen. We didn't hire a stand-up comedian to tell jokes and we did not have massive tickle sessions. All it took was giving a room full of women permission to just be themselves.

Have you heard the one about the . . .

I want to pause a minute to talk more about the importance of laughter, specifically when it comes to finding your power through playfulness. Laughter plays a crucial role in both emotional and physical well-being, and often acts like a natural release. It's very similar to an orgasm, believe it or not, because like orgasms, laughter involves the activation of the parasympathetic nervous system, which calms the body.[26]

But more importantly, laughter also connects people and it has always been a great tool women have used to build communities. Women are funny! Some say that women don't have a sense of humour (hmmm – I've never heard a woman say this): women are actually hilarious, and our humour often strengthens our connections. As a comedian (one of the many hats I wear) I've often been met with disapproval from men, who referred to my comedy as vulgar. It was never personal, I am aware of other female comedians being told that their humour is crass, an obvious double standard given how rude and unapologetic so many male comedians are who I doubt ever get told to "tone things down". Female comedians have had to balance their comedy with being cute in order to appeal to a mass market – harking back to the roles women played in society once upon a time, and the idea of women as delicate, polite, demure and, most of all, quiet. Because a woman standing on stage and talking about what fell out of her vagina after she gave birth, how many haemorrhoids she has or how cracked her nipples are after breastfeeding can send some men into a frenzy. Plus, telling women that we are not funny is another way to silence us. It sometimes is as simple as that, just as "gossip" became a rude word that oppressed women and discouraged us from talking to one another.

But it is through that raw humour and the funny stories we tell about our shared experiences – especially difficult ones, be it birth stories, snoring husbands, perimenopause symptoms, crappy dates and nasty bosses – that we connect, relate and encourage each other.

Of course, humour is more than just telling jokes. It's a way to push boundaries, to normalize things that people won't always talk about. It has always been a tool used in female groups. I think back to my mother with her girlfriends sitting around her kitchen table cackling loudly and I know that even in tough times when she or they were going through hardships, it was their ability to laugh *together* that made them stronger. Laughing when things are hard reminds you that it's going to be okay. Laughing with people you love gives you comfort and reassures you that you are not alone. I know from my interactions with so many women I've met, on the retreats and elsewhere, that finding their laughter again was the first step in reconnecting with that part of them they felt had been lost with age.

> ## SUGGESTION: FINDING FUN
>
> Make a list of things that give you joy and are pure fun. They can be anything from silly things like going to a karaoke club and singing your heart out, to planning a weekend away with your friends, playing board games, creating art, exploring nature or climbing trees.
>
> Do include in your list small things as well, stuff that feels more achievable, like going to see a comedy show or just dancing around your living room for no reason.
>
> The point is to write down things you know you would enjoy doing that can potentially bring out your less serious side and then do some of them! Start small and don't judge yourself. Set aside 5 to 15 minutes a day to do something playful. This practice should be enjoyable and not feel like hard work, so don't pressure yourself into doing anything you don't really want to!
>
> Also try to involve other people in your practice. Playing is always so much more fun when you play with others . . .
>
> Have fun!

Getting creative

I also think that playing is linked with creativity. Think about it, you can't be creative without playing if you are scared of making mistakes. The whole idea of playing is to let go of that fear of getting things wrong, and this is precisely what is at the heart of being creative. Imagine if artists were too scared of getting it wrong? We wouldn't have art in the world! Playing, like being creative, is about taking chances. It's about saying "F*ck it, I'm just gonna give it a go, and if I fail, I'll just try again." You can't play if you are being careful. Playing is about exploring and discovering, not about getting it right. Now imagine that was your state of mind with everything in life . . . how much more fun would life be?

Play acting

The other important element about playing is being in the moment – shutting out all the external noise, the to-do lists, the worries, the plans and all of the other things that often consume our brains (especially women's brains because, let's face it, they never stop!). I struggle to quieten my mind and while I'd love to say that I've mastered the art of meditation, that would be an absolute lie.

Instead, what has worked really well for me is *playing*.

When I started planning the retreats I knew that I wanted to bring some elements from my days as an actress into them, specifically my experience with improvisation. I had participated in many improvisation workshops over the years and they were always so much fun, I knew that even without having any acting experience, people would enjoy them. I also knew that if I told people we would be doing an improvisation workshop half of them wouldn't come. So I didn't. Instead I called the session "Play", which is effectively what improvising is.

The session was filled with games, starting with icebreakers and movement games then moving into vocal stuff and onto full make-believe scenarios, much like what you would see in a playground. It's incredible watching grown-ups pretend to be a pack of penguins, high on weed in a rave on the moon. But then again – why not? The first rule of improvisation is that there are no bad ideas. In fact, the two words most used during those sessions are "yes, and", which create a supportive environment of sharing and building on each other's ideas. We take what someone gives us and we add to it. We don't block.

FIND YOUR POWER THROUGH PLAYFULNESS

Imagine if we used this one simple tool in other areas of our lives!

For me improvisation enabled the quitting of my mind. The lack of time to think and plan, and the fact you have to jump in and just do and react, along with the supportive environment, allows you to be in your most ridiculous state, meaning that you are present, which is so rare with the constant stimulations of modern-day living. For me, playing is a brilliant tool to achieve a calm mind and, as an added bonus, it's so much fun.

I wasn't sure how people would react to the idea, but having done several of these workshops at my retreat and elsewhere, I have been so pleasantly surprised to see how much joy people take in playing like kids. It's so freeing.

***

In the Winnie-The-Pooh stories there is a line I really love about this idea: "But wherever they go, and whatever happens to them on the way, in that enchanted place on the top of the Forest, a little boy and his Bear will always be playing."[27] I want to believe that this is possible for all of us.

Life can get too serious if you don't let yourself have some fun from time to time, and who better to do it with than with other women?

While I can't give you an exact road map to finding your own playfulness, because your idea of fun might be different to mine, I am hoping that this will inspire you to look for it. You might be curious and sign up to a local improvisation class or dance club or head off to the bingo, look for something creative or a silly activity, or why not set up a playful evening with some friends to bring more fun into your lives. Whatever it is, the point is to open up to the idea of introducing playfulness into your life and to prioritize it. It's about giving yourself permission to be more than just the person in charge of making sure everyone else is having fun while you carry all the bags. It's about saying, "I want to have fun too" and finding the people in your life who you can do this with.

Girls' trip

A few years ago I went on an all-girls' trip to Ibiza with some close friends. It was one of the items on my then bucket list and the first girls-only trip I had gone on in years, and you can probably imagine how hard it was to arrange it. Everyone was busy, struggling with "mom guilt" and worried about leaving their husbands and children behind, so when we actually managed to find a weekend that everyone could make, it was nothing short of a miracle. I also don't need to tell you how much fun we had because I know you can picture it.

The three of us partied, ate amazing food, laid on the beach for hours while sipping cocktails, went shopping, slept in, got a massage, stayed up late gossiping and laughing our faces off till our cheeks hurt. It was rejuvenating, but from the inside. That thing you get when you spend time with girlfriends and you remember who you are. It was fun and funny and brilliant and exactly what we all needed.

I have not been back to Ibiza since, but I have gone away with my girlfriends several times since that trip and every time I do, I am better for it. We need our girlfriends to remind us of who we are under all our labels; we need the humour women bring, the lightness and the sisterhood to feel connected to ourselves. The fun I have with my girlfriends can't be compared to fun I have with anyone else, including my husband and children whom I love very much.

And if you need a little reminder of the potential for fun and playfulness when spending time with the gals, just think back to your school days, way, way before you became an adult/partner/parent, etc. I have vivid memories of sleepovers, giggling about boys, sharing crush stories, prank calls, school trips, swimming in lakes, hitting the beach, parties, new experiences and everything that comes with being young and free and surrounded by your friends. It was the perfect setting for having fun and being joyful, and it can be exactly that at any age.

Especially right now, if you let it.

There is a lot out there about the benefits of positive affirmations and I am sure you know what profound impact our inner dialogue has on our state of mind. I won't get into this too much but I will say this – what you say to yourself matters and you have the ability to bring more joy and playfulness into your life, simply by saying it! I invite you to try starting your day with that in mind. Can you make it a new habit when you wake up to think or even say out loud, "Today is going to be an amazing day!" or "Lots of fun things are going to happen to me!" or "I am excited about my day and I'm going to enjoy it." Anything along those lines sets you up for a day that has joy in it.

What I am trying to say is that the potential is almost always there, but if we don't look for it and aim to find it, sometimes it can pass us by.

Let's "gossip" about my therapist...

My husband and I started going to couples therapy, but people always assume the worst when you tell them that. It's like "Oh wow, are you guys okay? Are you getting a divorce? Are you going through a rough patch?" I don't know what they're talking about. As far as I am concerned, marriage IS a rough patch! I think of therapy like I think about exercising — no one really loves doing it, but it's good for you. So, yeah, just like people go to the gym to work out on their bodies, we go to couple's therapy to work on our relationship.

Anyway, I met Sofia, our therapist, and she was the first person to introduce me to the Japanese concept of "Ma" 間.

We were talking about how hectic our lives are and how, between the school run, meal planning and work, we barely had time for ourselves, let alone time for each other.

Sofia spoke about the philosophical concept of the space between the edges — a gap, a space or a pause. We talked about the importance of stopping to smell the flowers (it was more like a metaphor) and about how all the planning, rushing around and constant "doing" is driving us crazy and taking away our joy.

I sat there nodding because deep down I knew she was right — our day-to-day life often resembles a military operation that's trying to tackle a jam-packed schedule with no room for any mistakes. We reach the end of the day beat, tired and relieved the day has finally come to an end, only to realize that another hectic day awaits us around the corner, and the never-ending merry-go-round continues.

We needed to stop, but neither of us knew how. We have three young kids and a lot of our life revolves around them. Their education, their friendships, their hobbies, etc. How do we stop when life is speeding full force ahead?

Sofia recommended meditation, quiet time, reading a book, switching our phones off, walks on the beach, a weekend away, sitting in silence, and many other wonderful ideas. They all sounded great, but at the same time completely unachievable for a couple who have three kids in two different schools, two dogs, a large house that no matter how much you tidy it up always seems to be a mess, and two businesses to run.

I so desperately wanted to go on a walking meditation and find Ma, but instead of Ma all I could hear was "MOM!" and I was pulled back to fire-fighting, problem-solving, sock-finding. There was a moment when not being able to find the time to do yoga or breathe like Sofia suggested made me feel bad.

When Sofia talked about Ma, it felt like adding another task to my already full plate. Like now, on top of everything else, I also needed to make time for visualizations or repeating mantras. And then it hit me — what I needed was to get things OFF MY PLATE.

It's common to look at others and think, "Well, if everyone is doing it then it must be right", and while initially I knew I needed to slow down, everyone racing toward an invisible finish line confused me and made me want to go faster.

I haven't quite got the hang of meditating yet, but I did learn the fine art of saying "no" and doing less. And for me, that is my Ma.

I realize that I knew what I needed to do even before we started therapy, but for whatever reason, I didn't trust my own gut, and so it cost me a lot of money to realize what I knew all along.

CHAPTER FIVE
FIND YOUR POWER THROUGH FINDING YOUR WISDOM

Think about how you make decisions – and life seems full of them. How comfortable are you when faced with a dilemma? Do you trust your own judgement or do you lack confidence and question and doubt it? Is making a decision a tortuous experience? Do you drive yourself crazy over even the littlest of things? Are you scared of making the "wrong" choice, which means you often avoid making a decision? Are you seeking perfection and believe that for every decision you make there is one "correct" answer? Do you trust other people's wisdom over your own?

When I say "wisdom" in this chapter I'm talking about that intuition, that deep sense of knowing, a connection to nature and a calm assurance when making a choice. When I talked about wisdom in other places in the book I also referred to life experiences, stories, insights, etc, but for the purpose of this chapter, I'd like to focus more on intuitive knowledge. These qualities are unfortunately not rated in our society and often are even ridiculed or viewed as a weakness. It's not the type of learning you get in school. In fact, it could be said that schools, and other constraining environments that often stifle creativity and individuality, not only fail to encourage wisdom, but actively suck it right out of us. With formal learning, we are not taught to think for ourselves or trust ourselves, and are often encouraged to follow an official way of thinking.

Wisdom is *knowing* as opposed to driving yourself crazy trying to guess or over-research something. It's the ability to listen to your inner voice instead of other people's opinions. It is your intuition, that "I just know it" feeling that can't be explained. Women's wisdom has always been a powerful force, but it's one that's often been silenced and ignored. However, wisdom is hard to access because most of us don't have the space for it. In the chaos of modern life, with its demands and distractions, from "to-do lists" to the endless notifications, it can feel nearly impossible to find the quiet moments we need to connect with that deeper part of ourselves. But this disconnection isn't just a symptom of our busy lives – it's something rooted in history.

Wise woman or witch?

For centuries, women's collective knowledge has been oppressed. Our "wise women" forebears who used the natural world and traditional healing were powerful members of their communities, commanding respect and championing female knowledge and skills. Healers, and often midwives, were damned once medicine became a scientific concern around the time of the Renaissance. Studying and science were very much a male domain, and not accessible to women or those of the lower ranks of society. It was men and their "medicine" that drove many wise women to the stake, and it was not then far to go from the fear of "witches" to the dismissal of older women as "hags", "harridans" and "crones".[28] These archetypes were wise women, leaders of communities and holders of wisdom and protective powers. They weren't just feared, they were also mocked and even erased because they represented a kind of strength that couldn't be controlled.

FIND YOUR POWER THROUGH FINDING YOUR WISDOM

In today's society, learning and thinking is tightly controlled within a regulated, authorised structure.

But we are all unique and one of a kind, though, so how is it that in our society so many of the things we are taught are standardized? Imagine being free to follow your inner knowing, your own curiosity, and your intuition. Imagine you were taught to trust yourself. That instead of seeking wisdom in others, you were assured that it was already within you and that all you needed to do is listen. The textbook scholar version of "knowledge" is valued above all – and this can be damaging to our sense of self-belief and sense of self.

Of course, learning from others is essential. Shared wisdom, and generational wisdom in particular, are hugely valuable resources and points of reference, but when our self-trust is replaced by a lot of noise from the outside – and our words are abused and minimized with labels of "crazy" and "hysterical" and "over-emotional" – then we easily lose sight of who we are and our essential beliefs and original thoughts.

Talking of "hysterical" – are you aware that for hundreds of years, hysteria (from the Greek "hystera" for "uterus') was named as a mental disorder exclusive to women – another way to attempt control over and the silencing of women.[29] Common symptoms ranged from fainting and anxiety to an over or under-appetite for sex, irritability, and "a tendency to cause trouble for others". Men's attempts to diagnose and treat the "condition" – which they believed was linked to sex and either a "wandering uterus" around the body (I'm not joking) or too much retained fluid in the uterus – often involved marriage and sex. Lack of marriage was generally seen as the cause of much "melancholy" in women!

Honestly, the more you delve into the history of so many of these words that are used to describe women ("crazy", "hysterical", "gossip", etc) the more you realize how being called any of those words should really be taken as a compliment because it clearly means you're doing something right (and pissing a whole lot of people off)!

Out of touch with ourselves

I feel that one of the main reasons we are disconnected from our wisdom is because we live such busy lives. As women, we are constantly rushing, trying to do everything, be everywhere and achieve all things. Our lives consist of never-ending to-do lists that include careers, driving the kids around, working out, planning holidays, making appointments, grocery shopping, shaving our legs, packed lunches, etc. We try so hard to rise to the expectations society has placed on us to be sexy, educated, slim, healthy, motherly and successful, as well as drink green shakes, do Pilates and pelvic floor exercises, plan weekly date nights, have a great looking Instagram grid, take our supplements, never grow old, bake cupcakes – and, above all, be busy at all times.

Add the usual phone/social media addiction to the above and you are left with none of the moments of peace and quiet which happen to be where *wisdom* lives.

Wisdom is not a fast thing. It's not a trend or a catchy hit you hear on the radio. It's not fast food, or overconsumption, or doing as much in as little time as possible. It's not about getting places faster. It's not about being more efficient. It's not about making the most money. It's not about winning, or ticking items off a bucket list and it's not about listening to as many self-help books or improving podcasts as possible on double speed while you power walk.

Wisdom doesn't have FOMO. Wisdom isn't constantly trying to change things up. And most of all, wisdom is not complicated. It's simple.

In fact, wisdom *is* simplicity; like the old saying "less is more". Its rhyme is slow, it's filled with spaces, silences and time, and sometimes it's about doing nothing at all.

Making space

When I think about slowing down and making more space, I think about reconnecting – and how it's deeply linked to becoming more ourselves. Slowing down to feel, to be present, to be more aware of how we feel and who we are, and to understand what we truly want – all of these are connected. For me, it's so clear that living in a constant state of hurry pulls me away from my true self. If I'm always rushing, how can I possibly stay connected to my needs or my inner wisdom?

One interesting thing I've realized about myself, something you might relate to, is that this sense of urgency gave me the illusion of living a full and successful life. I was subconsciously taught that if you're busy and productive, you must be doing well. In fact, anything less was often labelled as "laziness", and that was presented as one of the worst things imaginable. Even today, I still feel uncomfortable when I'm not actively doing something. There's a voice somewhere in the back of my mind saying, "Don't be lazy, there's always something that needs doing – get up and do it!"

Even simple tasks, like grocery shopping, somehow turn into stressful events because I rush through them in a small window of time – just another consequence of stretching myself too thin. And I often wonder: beyond being a habit and a norm in Western culture, is this urgency also a way to avoid thoughts and feelings we'd rather not confront? If I'm too busy to slow down, reflect or sit with my emotions, maybe I can avoid feeling hurt. I don't know for sure.

But what I do know is this: one day, as I was hurrying my kids to go to the park to "have fun" (on a weekend, no less!), one of my daughters looked at me and asked, "Mommy, why are you always in a rush?" And in that moment, I realized something important – it was a choice I was making.

Sure, I had convinced myself it was a necessity. We had a lot to do that day and I wanted to get to the park while it was still sunny, etc. But in reality, that wasn't entirely true.

I had chosen to overbook myself, to commit to a schedule that left no breathing room so that we only had a short window of opportunities to go to the park. And just as I had chosen to run on empty for so long, I could also choose to do things differently.

In short, I realized that *slowing down is a choice I can make*.

"Stuffocation"

Our culture of overconsumption has a lot to answer for. We overbuy and fill our houses with stuff we don't need. When something breaks, we get a new one. We scroll online late at night and find ourselves ordering air fryers, juicers and other "extras" we use once or twice and then store on a top shelf and forget all about. We buy fast fashion, our houses and brains are cluttered with piles of throwaway stuff no one remembers getting and, while feeling overwhelmed with having too many things to do and too little time to do it might not seem connected, it is in fact very much part of the problem. Not only is our "space" consumed, but the concept of the importance and value of things is lost.

Big house, big problems. Lots of stuff, lots of problems. You get the idea.

The more stuff we have, the bigger house we need; the bigger house we need, the more time we need to spend on maintaining it and the more we need to work to afford it. It's a vicious cycle.

And it's not just the excess stuff or the ample options that are adding complexity to our lives, it's also the quest for "the best" option, rather than the easiest one or the good enough one or the local one. The one that's less flashy but does the job just fine. In short, often the abundance of unnecessary stuff clutters our brains and serves as a destruction that prevents us from tuning into our wisdom.

Female knowledge

Throughout history, women's wisdom, knowledge and contributions across medicine, philosophy, science, literature, music, art and all aspects of life have been ignored and overlooked – and lost to those generations that followed. Societal norms and patriarchal structures confined women to domestic spheres, and educational and legal restrictions restrained their wisdom. Again, it's shocking to think about how recently this man-washing of history was still occurring – can you name a female composer, artist, scientist or philosopher pre-1950? History was written by men, for men, about men. And we are still fighting to adjust the education our children receive about what has gone before.

There are so many women I could write about that throughout history were mocked and ignored – women who had knowledge, talent and extraordinary abilities to offer. The list is too long to name them all but I have no doubt that we as a society have missed out on so much because of gender inequality. There is finally a resurgence in uncovering women whose names should be known far and wide, and rewriting the histories of many disciplines with these wise and talented women noted, but we shouldn't have to fight to uncover the wise women that have gone before. Read the *Good Night Stories for Rebel Girls* books,[30] *A History of the World with the Women Put Back In*[31] and *The Story of Art without Men*[32] and spread the word.

In 1842, the British mathematician Ada Lovelace wrote one of the first algorithms intended to be executed by a machine – essentially the first computer program. Unfortunately, her contributions were largely overshadowed by her male collaborator, Charles Babbage, and her work wasn't fully recognized until a century later. Sculptor Camille Claudel's immense talent was similarly dismissed until more recently, obscured by the work of her lover, Rodin. We should be far more aware of Margaret Sanger, the unorthodox nurse who we should thank for the legalization of contraception. The brilliant mathematician and physicist Katherine Johnson's name became more widely known with the publication of her story, and that of her NASA African-American female mathematician colleagues, in *Hidden Figures* (and the subsequent Oscar-winning film). Read up on the women that history didn't bother to record, and be aware of these and the many, many more women out there across all fields of knowledge and creativity who worked with them.

We are living in a world that hasn't fully benefited from what female knowledge and wisdom can offer. Take a moment to think about that. When I see all the negative things in our world – wars, poverty, environmental damage, etc – I often wonder what the world would look like if more women had been and were now involved in the decision making.

Listening to our own wisdom

For many of us, the natural connection to our intuition, our inner voice and wisdom, has been lost, and instead we've replaced it with colour-coordinated Excel spreadsheets and pros-and-cons lists. We have stopped listening to our hearts because we were told that we need to be led by our head. While I am very connected to my analytic brain and love a hard fact, as well as examining any problem or dilemma through rational thinking, research and long conversations with literally everyone I know, I have come to see how overthinking adds stress to my life and how sometimes going with my gut has proven to be the best course of action. It is very common for women to drive themselves crazy making choices or doing a task (like booking a family holiday, for example) while trying to keep everyone (except ourselves) happy. It takes years off our lives!

In our modern way of living there is real pressure to get things "right". It's a misleading premise that for every decision there is a "right" and "wrong" choice. Imagine how stressful that type of thinking is! So every time we are faced with any type of dilemma, whether it's about what school to send our kids to, a big move, a change in career, etc – we go into the decision thinking that we have to choose "right", and that if we don't it will be catastrophic. It causes anxiety and for some people is the main reason they avoid making decisions at all.

I am sure I don't need to tell you that it's rare that there is a right or wrong decision. Life is just full of options: for every choice you make, you simply take a different route. I heard a story about Barack Obama talking about decision making. He was asked how he'd learned to become good at making decisions, and he explained that, as President, he'd only ever been faced with truly difficult and exceptional decisions. "Easy" decisions would have been made by someone else, before it landed on his desk. If there was an obvious answer, then it wouldn't have reached him. Once he understood the concept that the decision didn't have a "right" or "wrong" answer, and that he would just have to make the best decision he could at that time, then it became easier to appreciate that there would be positive and negative outcomes from the decision, and that he could only do the best possible with the information available.

It's a bit like that movie *Sliding Doors* with Gwyneth Paltrow – we have lots of different paths we can follow and we just have to make a choice and see where it leads. I like to think of making a decision as actually taking power back rather than letting our lack of choice make the decision for us, or leaving us in limbo and losing out from the lack of decision.

Many of us also avoid making mistakes for fear we might be judged. But if I have learnt anything in my 49 years, it is that people will judge you no matter what you do, so you might as well give them something to talk about!

Generational wisdom

When I think of female wisdom I immediately think about generational wisdom because it encompasses the collective knowledge and insight women have developed and passed down through generations. From grandmother to mother, from mother to daughter, the wisdom women have shared with one another has guided communities and families, fostered cultural heritage, preserved traditions and kept family stories alive, giving people a better understanding of where they came from. This generational knowledge is a combination of practical information, moral values and life skills and it all helps with providing a sense of identity. Ultimately, the flow of wisdom between generations, which is primarily by women, was and is a source of great power.

I will never forget the stories my grandmother told me about how she shared a home with her mother and mother-in-law (you heard correctly) and how much she loved it. While my grandfather spent days away from home working, together with these other two women, she would cook, look after the kids, sing, dance, share stories about the "good old days" back in the far away lands they each came from, and support each other in the daily challenges. My grandmother was a young mother and found great comfort in having these two older women by her side, guiding her and teaching her from their experience. I know that for many the idea of living with your mother and mother-in-law is the definition of an absolute nightmare, but my grandmother looked back at the time she had with them with great love and appreciation. Years later, after they were both gone and with my grandfather also passed away, my grandmother felt very lonely. All the kids had grown up and moved away and the house felt empty. She loved reminiscing though and when I would visit she would make us tea and tell me her stories. Her eyes would gaze toward the empty living room as she described the hustle of a full house of kids and larger-than-life women who were loud and had lots of opinions, and she would smile. Although I never met either of them, she made me understand what that friendship and community had meant to her and given her.

Over time, however, we have shifted toward a more individualistic society and female wisdom has lost its value. In the past, living in close-knit communities meant that families shared not just a home but also wisdom, knowledge, and stories. Grandmothers played a crucial role in passing down life lessons, traditions, etc and everyone learned from one another in an organic way. It was often the physical closeness of living together that allowed wisdom to be shared so easily.

As modern society developed, things started to change. People moved away from home for study or work, technology advanced and travel became easier, and so living near your family or even spending a lot of time with them became less and less common. Suddenly elders didn't have the same space to share their knowledge, and younger generations grew up more isolated from those life lessons with other people and sources becoming the source of information and wisdom – like social media and influencers, for example.[33]

I think it's important to recognize that while modern life has brought a lot of positives, this is another very valuable practice that has been lost along the way.

Ghosted elders

Perhaps linked to that breakdown in generational living, we are now part of a world that idealizes and celebrates youth, while older women are looked at as irrelevant and expected to disappear into the shadows at the age of 50. I certainly felt a shift in how I was viewed when I hit my mid-40s. It was almost as if there was a silent understanding that you become invisible. It's interesting that, as women come out of the childbearing stage, and once again want to "take up space", have opinions and care less about what others think of them, that is when many women are portrayed as mad, hysterical, crazy and out of touch. It's as if they don't want us to tap into our feminine power so we get pushed to the side, labelled as irrelevant.

This attitude toward older women is sometimes masked as something else – for example, when people give women over 50 "compliments" like "You look great for your age" or "Still rocking it at 50". They subtly shift the focus to the idea that aging is something women must overcome to still be relevant. Negative attitudes toward mothers, and particularly mothers-in-law, are another great example. If you tell someone they are turning into their mother, it is always considered an insult – but why? There's a general perception of women aging into out-of-touch, doddery, interfering characters – not exactly the venerated wise women of the past. And think of the "mother-in-law" jokes and tropes that are standard – again, why do we demonize older women so easily?

How and when does that happen? When we are little we adore our mothers and perceive them as perfect, and while it's normal to grow up and see your parents as flawed individuals who made mistakes, it's very strange how much of an insult taking after one's mother is considered in our society. (There are not the same connotations if you tell a man they are becoming like their dads.) How convenient it is for some to slot older women into the "mother-in-law" position, to label them as overbearing and someone to distance yourself from. Also think about how this is used to divide women of different stages/generations and limit the knowledge and support that could flow between women.

The misogyny and the general hatred our patriarchal society has toward older women is a common thread throughout most Western societies. Once you age (and motherhood is part of that), you are largely ridiculed and/or ignored. As your role and function in society adjusts from child-rearer, you are sidelined from public life. Again, it's not the same for men – Susan Sontag called this out as the "double standard of aging" in 1978. Social media is filled with jokes about middle-aged women who complain about stuff. (Today people refer to a "Karen" – originally a term for racist white woman – which has become a general term used to describe a white woman with an opinion and is often used to shut women up.) I know women who are embarrassed to be "middle aged" only because of the negative association linked to it. We see men "aging gracefully" while women "let themselves go". Men's silver hair is celebrated but women's silver hair is a topic of conversation. Many women are body shamed for their "mom bods" while "dad bods" are revered as sexy.

But I have come to see how all of that is a lie. I have come to see how women get so much better with age. The calm that comes with getting older, with knowing your worth, knowing who you are is something I would choose a million times over being young again. I know a lot of people get really stressed out over getting old, and for women this feels even more challenging. I have friends dreading turning 30, 40 or 50 like their lives are going to be over when they reach that round number. But a smart woman once told me that the most meaningful years aren't the milestone birthdays themselves, but the year leading up to them. She said, "When you turn 50, you're actually celebrating the end of your 50th year - which, when you think about it, isn't all that exciting. But when you turn 49, you're stepping into your 50th year, entering a whole new decade - and that's where the magic happens." I know she was right because I feel how this year (as I am about to turn 50) is carrying huge shifts, movement and transformation for me. I feel more myself now as I am about to enter my 50s than I did in my 20s and 30s, and even my 40s, which were pretty amazing. And so to anyone else experiencing this, all I can suggest is that you embrace it, celebrate it, and step into whatever new chapter that's about to come with excitement. And if you are in doubt, find older women to talk to. I bet a lot of them will tell you from experience that it only gets better.

When I was writing my recent stand-up show, one of the gags was about how Mike said to me one day that I was becoming more and more like my mother and how upset I was to hear that. When I read the section to my 13 year old she asked, "But why were you upset?"

And that's when it hit me.

Pass it on

My mother was far from a perfect mother, but she did her best with the resources she had. I don't remember my mother sitting me down and sharing her wisdom with me, possibly because no one did that with her, but I did learn a lot from her. What's interesting to note though is *what* we learn from the women in our lives. My mom for example gave me my first razor and taught me how to shave my legs. She taught me how to cook and how to sing. She took me to the gynaecologist when I started having sex so that I could get the pill. She told me that getting my highlights at a salon would be more effective than squeezing lemons on my head. She taught me how to drive and how to love chocolate. She also taught me how to diet and how to hate my body, not intentionally but simply because she hated her own. She taught me many things she had learnt herself from living in a patriarchal system and, like a lot of women, she did pass on wisdom, but it wasn't always female wisdom. None of this is surprising when I think of her and her generation of women facing different opportunities and attitudes both at work and at home – but at a cost.

Many of our mothers were not connected to their female wisdom any more than we are, and so how could they pass it on to us? Maybe no one taught you about your cycle and how to track it or what female hormones meant. Not many mothers talk to their daughters about pleasure, setting boundaries or listening to their needs, because many of them are not aware of their own pleasure and needs. Many mothers don't teach their daughters how to be free and fearless because they are not free and fearless themselves. Many mothers don't know how to "mother" in a way that allows the lineage of generational wisdom because they did not have a role model for how to do it. They were taught how to be women through the male gaze and they taught us that instead.

As a mother I think a lot about what I would like to teach my own daughters. I know I don't have all the answers and I know that I am not getting it all right. There are still many areas in my life that I am working on. But in my opinion life is about the journey and not about reaching a point in time where we feel "This is it". So instead of trying to have all the answers for my kids, I try to teach them to listen to themselves. It wasn't something I've always done and what doesn't come naturally to you is hard to teach others. A cycle of distrusting your own inner voice that has been passed down from previous generations is hard to break. But I hope that as I get better doing this myself, I will also be teaching my children to do so too.

SUGGESTION: FINDING SPACE FOR WISDOM

Start by asking yourself if you have space in your life for wisdom? Do you have any gaps in your day where you can meditate, or go on a mindful walk without your phone or any agenda and just let your brain have some time off? If not, why? Bear in mind that space doesn't have to be massive. You don't need to take hours out of your busy day – we all work and have responsibilities and it's unlikely we

> can go off for hours. But despite the business and roles we play in our day-to-day lives, most of us have opportunities for space.
>
> Ten minutes a day is a great place to start.
>
> See if you can create space in your life to allow wisdom to come in. This can be as simple as a few minutes when you wake in the morning before jumping out of bed, just lay there with your eyes closed and focus on your breathing. Or try a mindful walk without any distractions (leave your phone at home). It could be a guided meditation just before you go to sleep.
>
> When faced with decisions, big or small, see what happens if you allow yourself more time to sit with the dilemma, rather than jump into action. Calming your mind will allow you to access your intuition and make better decisions. There isn't one way to do this – you can meditate, listen to music, take a long walk in nature – do whatever calms you down and gives you some space from the dilemma itself. This often allows you to see things from a different perspective and not make rash decisions based on fear or pressure.

The importance of generational relationships became clear to me during my second retreat where we had women in their late 60s sitting side-by-side with women in their early 20s. At first I didn't know how these two age groups would relate to each other, but as the days went by I got to see the most beautiful flow of knowledge and wisdom between women of all ages. What surprised me more than anything was that it flowed in all directions. While I had assumed that it would be the older women "teaching" the younger women, the transfer of wisdom was mutual. This showed me that everyone has wisdom to offer, no matter their age or the stage in life they are at. We all have something to teach, just like we all have something to learn.

To counter society's negative attitude toward female wisdom, we must challenge gender stereotypes and welcome the contributions of older women and their wisdom into our collective consciousness. Look for ways to foster intergenerational connections because when women come together, they create a supportive network that amplifies their strengths. The insights from our mothers and grandmothers hold immense value; they enrich our own lives and strengthen our communities. I will return to this in the next chapter when I talk about finding your power through other women, but for now let's focus on the understanding that we all have wisdom in us, we just need to unleash it.

Let's "gossip" about Grace...

I moved to London just before my 30th birthday to pursue a career in acting. I auditioned and got into a well-known drama school in the city and did an MA course in Performing Arts which was my real first taste of acting.

When I started drama school I was so insecure. I hardly believed I deserved to be there. Toward the end of the year we had an opportunity to perform two monologues in front of a panel of casting agents and directors. Our teachers said this would be a good chance to experience what an audition would feel like and also explained that they might even end up casting us in one of their upcoming productions if we were lucky.

Like everyone else in my class, I prepared for weeks. I memorized the text, worked on my character, practised in front of the mirror and did everything we had been taught to do.

And then my moment came.

I stepped into the room and stood in front of the panel and... I choked.

I mean, I did the monologues, I remembered all the words and it wasn't awful, but it wasn't great either. I knew it and they knew it.

When I finished, there was an embarrassing silence in the room and then one of the panel cleared their throat and said, "Thank you, that was lovely, please send the next person in."

I walked out knowing I had blown it, but what was most frustrating is that I knew I had it in me to be amazing but I didn't take it. You see, throughout the year, our drama teacher had talked to us about the idea of "fight or flight". In those moments when you're on stage and you feel like you might throw up and your nerves might get the better of you, believe it or not — you have a choice. You can either succumb to "flight", which means you give in to your fears and do not allow yourself to take up all the space you were born to take, OR "fight", which means you go for it with every single fibre in your body.

As I walked out of the room it was clear to me what had happened — I had given up. I gave in to that little voice in my head that kept telling me I didn't deserve to be there. I was gutted.

Waiting to go in next was Grace, and she was looking really nervous.

"How did it go?" she asked.

I grabbed hold of her shoulders and I said, "Listen. Don't make the mistake I just made. I blew it! I didn't believe in myself and it showed. Don't do that, you go in there and give them your best, you hear me! Go in there and fight for it like your life depends on it. Do not be apologetic — fight!"

The door opened and Grace was called in. I could hear her delivering her monologue with confidence and when she finished everyone clapped. She was later cast in a West End production by one of the watching agents.

Since that experience, whenever I have doubts or fears that threaten to get the best of me, I give myself that exact same pep talk I gave Grace all those years ago.

CHAPTER SIX
FIND YOUR POWER THROUGH OTHER WOMEN

How do you feel about female friendships? Do they feel like a warm hug and a source of comfort and strength, or do they stir up fears of cattiness or competition? If the idea feels complicated, it might be worth reflecting on where those feelings come from. Did something specific happen that shaped your perspective or could it be tied to how society often portrays female friendships as dramatic or cut-throat? Now think about your own life: would you like to have more women around you? Do you find it easy to connect with other women? Who do you look up to in your relationships with women? Maybe it's a mentor, a teacher, or even an older friend who embodies wisdom and support. Take a moment to reflect on these ideas.

Our relationships with other women – old and young, family and friends, at all stages of life – are key to enabling us to be more open and awake to our essential selves and to shed our labels; they are at the core of this book. When I started on social media, my videos at first were all about motherhood and what I wanted – more than just venting and telling the world how close I was to losing my shit – was to let women know that if they felt the same way, it wasn't just them. If women are not connecting and talking to one another, how can we possibly know that what we're experiencing is normal?

And when I say "normal" I acknowledge that there is no such thing – what is normal for one person might not be the case for someone else. I guess that when I say "normal" I mean part of the experience (which basically can be anything); even if it's wild, it doesn't matter! I knew that my videos were making women laugh or feel better about themselves, and many of them even said they felt as if I was speaking directly to them and it was like gossiping with a best friend.

The move from traditional and smaller in-person communities that women used to have in the past to online massive communities marks a huge change in how women relate to each other, form female bonds, and communicate around changes in society. While parenting advice was always available, once upon a time this advice was passed down from mothers to daughters in smaller, more intimate settings, where there was also hands-on help offered and actual support. Today, however, many women lack that sense of community and don't have the same family support, so they turn online where they find communities that offer advice, but lack the one-on-one interactions in the "real world", and this can be problematic.

Don't get me wrong, I took great comfort in my own online community which I created when the kids were little. It was so validating hearing from women all over the world that I wasn't alone. That I wasn't crazy. And I know that it gave many others a sense of belonging that they lacked and desperately needed. But it's not the same as sitting in a room filled with other women who offer you a hug or to hold your baby so that you can take a shower. It's not the same as having a laugh with other women in person, or having them show you how to do something you find hard. It's not the same as having a good old natter with your girlfriends in person. It's just no comparison.

Making a move

In 2022 my husband Mike and I decided to leave the UK and move to Portugal. The decision came after he unexpectedly lost a close friend to a rare disease and the two years of Covid had crystallized just how fragile life really was. Living in London was alright on paper: we had our own home, the kids went to a decent school, we were both working and we were able to walk to the Heath from our house. We were grateful for it, but neither of us was really enjoying ourselves. Life felt like a rat race, only we were too scared of what it would mean to stop it.

So we carried on.

At the same time I was feeling that my social circle had shrunk. One of my closest friends had moved out of London, another went back to her home country and the little pack of women I had cultivated for years simply did not exist anymore. What I am trying to say is that, despite the nice house, husband, kids and job, I was ready for a change.

One day after I had done the school run, picked up something for dinner and done the millionth load of laundry for that week, I turned to Mike and said, "Let's leave London."

The idea was that life was too short to wait till we retired to settle down somewhere sunny by the coast or take up whatever future hobby we thought we might have in our 60s or 70s. Life is happening *now* and no one is guaranteed any future, so why not take all the risks while we can still remember each other's names.

This thought brought us to Portugal – hardly an extreme change in lifestyle, being a country in Western Europe with a massive expat community – but it felt like a big change for us as a family and just the right amount of reshuffling we needed.

Funnily enough, and totally unexpectedly, Portugal brought so many new women into my life. I have made some incredible friends in the short space of time we've been here, many of which I would have probably never met had we not moved. And while deep friendships take years to build, being part of an international community in a country that is away from home for all of us, has meant that those friendships deepen much faster. We are each other's support system because none of us has family or people we've known since childhood here. We are all in the same boat – brand new and eager to make friends. In the two years since moving I have come to recognize again the importance of having other women in my life. They are there when I need to vent or to have a laugh and gossip, there to help with the kids, there to share holidays, or go on vacations together with. I have learnt something from each and every one of them, through the conversations we have had about our lives, about other people in our lives and just from being together. I honestly wouldn't be having such a great experience living in Portugal if it wasn't for the women I've met and become close friends with. They are a massive part of my life here and if ever we decided to return to the UK they would be what I'd miss most.

Women's circles

I love reading about and creating women's circles – there can never be enough! Historically, they obviously centred around the natural world, often ceremonial and honouring the moon, and celebrating the feminine. There would have been a fire, and stories, and teachings and probably singing and dancing. They were about bonding and healing and being present with other women.[34] A resurgence in recent times calls out the need for women to be together – whether it's about wicca or knitting, manifesting or baking. I've taken part in many circles and some have been Shamanic ceremonies, some were singing with drums, and it always amazes me how little you actually need to make a deep connection. One of the things I've loved the most is the sharing part – listening to women say how supported they feel just by being surrounded by women is a recurring theme.

When we got to Portugal I had just come out of two intense years of working in isolation. Covid meant that my entire operation was now online and I was suffocating. I longed for human connection, especially with other women, so I decided to start running Female Empowerment Retreats in the Algarve as a way to meet the incredible women who had been following me on social media for years. The idea was to offer a few days of pampering and fun in a beautiful setting but what came out of these retreats was something I could have never expected or planned.

It was clear from day one at retreat number one that we had created something special. That when women come together, it is special. And also, that women everywhere were "starving", living in isolation without a female community, and so when they had a space to come together, they absolutely exploded.

Ahead of the retreat I sourced amazing facilitators and put together a programme that covered a range of different topics I was passionate about which were all intended to "empower". Many of those topics can be found in this book. I knew the programme was solid and I had no doubt the women would find value in what I created for them, but what I hadn't expected was how much value they would find in simply being with each other and how much value *I* would find in witnessing it all.

On the first day of the first retreat we sat in a circle – the first women's circle I had done in a while and, within seconds, magic happened. The first few people who spoke said a very brief introduction, who they were, how old, why they came and then, around about when the fourth or fifth person spoke, everything changed.

She began speaking about a personal struggle of hers and I could feel the vibe changing. Everyone's body changed, they all leaned in and the energy shifted. There was a sense of familiarity, of "We've been here before, we know this, we are in it together." After that everyone opened up. There were tears and laughter, and above all there was listening and so much empathy.

Stronger together

It's something I work on because my instinct is to solve. My default is to try and make things better. My "go to" is *doing*. I used to tell my friends, "Come to me when you're ready to do something about it."

The retreats changed that.

It was refreshing and frankly rather shocking seeing how something as simple as sitting in a circle where everyone can see each other had the ability to transform. That openess, the allowing each other to just be, was like the sign everyone needed. I could see women who had held on to a harsh exterior, the bit that tells them not to cry because they might be called emotional or hysterical, suddenly softened.

It's not just the physical sitting together obviously, it's the creation of a space for women where they feel safe to shed their masks and armours and to be themselves. To be seen and to be witnessed is something we rarely get to do.

Life teaches us to toughen up. To add layers so that we don't get hurt. To grow thicker skin to defend ourselves. To learn how to adapt and hide ourselves in order to fit in. All of these skills are important for survival in our fast-paced competitive world, but they also come at a price.

Women's circles create a safe space for us to share ourselves fully and have others listen to us, not try to solve anything, but rather to *be there* for each other – and it is immensely powerful. The act of "witnessing" alone has tremendous healing potential. It creates a space for emotional release, safety and empathy. When people are seen in their vulnerability, it fosters connection, diminishes shame, and helps them integrate their experiences, leading to personal transformation.

And if I could give women and girls only one piece of advice in this whole book it would be to find and/or create women circles that you can be part of.

In that first circle on that first retreat, and in all the circles we've done since, women spoke openly about everything: relationships, grief, body image, sex, self-esteem, confidence, anxiety, depression, ambitions, successes, love, shame, motherhood, passion, work and more. They shared ideas, insights, inspirations, stories, lessons they'd learned, secrets, fears and dreams.

Being seen

One of the things that stood out the most to me is the power of being witnessed. I hadn't heard that term before my retreats and it was my lead facilitator Chiara who brought it to my attention. My understanding of this concept is that when we are witnessed, especially when we share our traumas and difficulties, by an empathetic receiver who does not judge us, it helps us heal.

Our instinct as people is to try and fix things and solve problems, and this includes when we see people suffering and in pain. We want to comfort them, give them advice and somehow make it all better and take away their pain. I think that deep down we also want to take away our own discomfort in those moments. It's not easy seeing people suffer. For many it feels awkward and we don't know what to do with ourselves. I also think we're not taught what to do in those situations. Think about all the times you were encouraged to stop crying or not to be sad when you were little. How much space was your discomfort allowed to have? Even as parents this is something we instinctively do with our own kids. I am guilty of this just like the next mom. Not gonna lie, it's hard for me to see my children suffer and the first thing I want to do is fix it for them.

But a lot of important things happen in those moments of discomfort.

I never would have thought that just sitting there in a circle of women and actively listening without judgement could help anyone in their healing journey, and when I started participating in these circles I felt very uncomfortable not doing anything when someone shared something that was painful or hard for them to share. Then I saw how much people took away from being able to speak freely about something that was hard for them without anyone trying to fix their discomfort. Just letting them be in that unpleasant state for as long as they needed was really powerful. They didn't need to say sorry for bringing the mood down like we often feel we need to do when we are sad. They didn't scare anyone away with their "ugly" sides. They were able to showcase their insecurities and be vulnerable and receive support and love from the rest of the group without any judgement, and that was freeing, empowering and transformative for many of them.

Women together

It's not easy to tap into that because women are frequently portrayed as envious of each other and in competition. Back when society largely defined a woman's success by whether she could marry and settle down, this idea fuelled a sense of rivalry among women. Thankfully, times have changed, but, even though we've made progress, traces of that old narrative still linger. It's like cultural residue – a leftover idea that we're slowly shaking off but that sometimes rears its head in subtle ways.

Take movies for example, when two women are cast opposite each other they are either each other's nemesis (*The Devil Wears Prada, Mean Girls, Death Becomes Her* come to mind), or one of them plays the lead while the other is the best friend "wing woman" (*Legally Blonde, Princess Diaries, Pitch Perfect*, etc). It's almost hard to imagine two brilliant women who don't hate each other, right? But the women in my life have never been the background to my life, nor have

FIND YOUR POWER THROUGH OTHER WOMEN

they been in competition with me. They have not been my sidekicks but rather an integral and main part of my story. And they have been leads, right there besides me.

Our female friends are the witnesses of our lives. They are our circle. Throughout our lives they are the ones who show up, listen, laugh, keep us company, support and grow with us. Our female friends are there for us through breakups, house moves, new jobs, new loves, heartbreaks, illnesses, new adventures, pregnancies and fashion disasters. They add the flavour, the richness, like a delicious main course – and are an integral part of our lives who make it so much better!

Let's "gossip" about Helen...

I met Helen a few years ago at a pole dancing class in London. She was the woman at the back who was hiding behind everyone else and dancing like a magical fairy. Something about her was so engaging, and I hoped to see her again. I was happy when she showed up the following week. She was still clinging on to her space at the back of the room, this time with a little smirk on her face, like she had a secret that was amusing her. I really wanted to know what it was!

Over the next few weeks I got to know Helen a little better, and then one evening after class was over we went out for a drink and she told me her story.

Apparently, Helen loved to dance when she was a little girl but her parents told her it was a sin.

Many girls are told that enjoying their bodies is a sin — it's one of the main reasons why so many women feel such deep shame about their own bodies and sexuality. Our bodies are often seen as tools for men's pleasure or for making babies, so when Helen danced as a child, an activity she enjoyed immensely, her parents punished her and told her to stop.

Helen carried on her life, she got a degree, got married, got a job, had kids and lived a good life, but while many things in her life made her happy — her family, her friends, work, etc — she missed that same level of pleasure she felt when she danced freely as a child.

Then about a month before I met Helen, she came across an ad on Facebook for a pole dancing class for beginners in her local area. She didn't think much of it until it popped up again on her feed and she thought it might be a sign, so she mustered up the courage to sign up for a free session.

On the way to the class she told herself how ridiculous it was for her, a 40-something-year-old woman, to take up pole dancing, but every time she thought she would turn back, something in her made her carry on.

It was fascinating seeing Helen's transformation over the next few months. While she never quite left her corner at the back, the pure joy and pleasure she felt when she danced was mesmerizing and would fill the whole space. In that room, in that corner, Helen allowed herself to feel pleasure and to be free.

CHAPTER SEVEN
FIND YOUR POWER THROUGH PLEASURE

What do you think about when you hear the word "pleasure". What pops into your mind? Does it have to do with food? Or being at a special place? Your body? Is it sexual? Touch? Or enjoying music or dance? What type of feeling does the word emote? Is it joy and indulgence? Or is it shame and guilt? Maybe it's a bit of both or maybe it's nothing at all? Think about what that might say about how your system sees/senses pleasure – as a negative/burdening/embarrassing/exciting/desired thing? Do you have pleasure in your life? If not, why do you think that is? Would you like to? How does pleasure fit into your life – is it a "need" for you?

When I think about pleasure I think about something physical. The first place my mind goes to is sexual pleasure (but that might just be me). Having said that, I can also get a lot of pleasure from having a bath, from dancing, even from eating a delicious cake!

Pleasure can cover a breadth of mental states, from happiness and enjoyment to entertainment and ecstasy. It's a one-time hit that generates a good feeling. It can often be bought with money, and the good feeling usually wears off when the activity expires. For me, it is something that's tangible – although it's a feeling, it is also often associated with something physical.

When I started thinking about my needs, physical needs were the first things that came to mind. From things like sleep and rest to nourishing my body and taking time for myself, I slowly started to see that I had completely ignored my needs for years, and the associated absence of pleasure. My days were a big rush, with very few moments of pure joy, or even enough space to just bask in whatever fun thing I might have been doing. Whether I was hanging out with my children or driving past a beautiful view, I couldn't find the pleasure in any of it. In other words, I might have been engaging in enjoyable stuff, but because I was already thinking about the next place I had to be or all the things I still had to do, I wasn't feeling or finding pleasure in anything.

Modern-day living isn't designed for pleasure, which I know might sound odd given that technology and progress have seemingly meant things take less time to do so in theory we should all have more time to do things that give us pleasure. But in reality, progress has meant our long "to-do lists" have grown even longer, and this is even more true for the burden that often falls to women. A lack of time is part of the issue – something that we tackle in several chapters in the book as it's linked to many ways to be more intentional in the choices we make about our lives.

It's the small things

When people are faced with the question "Do you have pleasure in your life?" they often think about big things. You might think about a massage with two therapists and warm oil all over your body, or maybe what comes to mind is a multiple orgasm after a three-hour session of hot tantric sex. You might think about a lavish holiday somewhere tropical or a tasting menu dinner prepared by a famous chef in a fancy restaurant.

While those ideas do sound very pleasurable, they are less achievable for most people because they take up time, they cost a lot of money and are not accessible to everyone – but it's actually the small pleasures that I'd like you to focus on for now. Sometimes it's the little things that can make all the difference. As an example, take that first coffee of the day, (it might be a tea for you, or a glass of orange juice – whatever your first morning drink is). The secret is – *how* you drink it.

Do you half-drink it as you rush to get the kids ready, pack their lunch boxes, feed the dog, then it's gone cold so you rarely even finish it. OR do you savour it? Do you sit down to drink it slowly and enjoy it? Do you grind fresh coffee beans and froth your milk? Do you make it into a ritual or do you just gulp it down as you rush out of the door?

I used to be the first type – I would make a tea and then barely drink it because I would get so distracted with the chaos of the morning, I would take a few sips and then find it hours later, cold and horrible.

But on the days when I had more intention to find pleasure, I would look for it, even in the little things – and I would allow myself to enjoy them. On those days I would sit down, sip my tea slowly, enjoying it and take my time. In fact, what I started doing was to wait to drink my tea until after the kids had gone to school so that no one could disturb me. Some days I even went outside, closed the door and soaked in the sun and, honestly, it was such a pleasure.

Something that simple, nothing huge – just a good cup of tea with the sun on your face – can be a moment of bliss.

Here, the awareness was key, rather than the actual activity itself, because pleasure can actually be found everywhere and it's not so hard to achieve.

It can be soaking in a bath with oils while the dishes wait in the sink and just enjoying the warmth of the water on your body. It can be a walk in the forest with the smell of fresh rain and nothing but the sound of birds around you. It can be drinking hot chocolate at the beach at sunset. It can be cuddling with your children on the sofa. It can be dancing in the kitchen while doing the dishes. It can be sex on a Tuesday night, or using your new vibrator. And the great thing is that most of these cost very little and are quite easy to achieve – they are small luxuries in life if we can make them happen.

The secret is to give yourself permission to take that little extra time to do whatever it is that you enjoy doing, and give it the attention it deserves. The two important things here are: intention and permission. Intention is another thing we don't naturally do because our hectic lives often mean we just hop from one thing to another and our goal is to finish as many tasks as possible. But what if we changed the goal and made it – pleasure? What if you were told that the point was not to complete a task fast, but rather to do it in a fun way? The intention is different, right?

Ask yourself: are you just ticking items off your "to-do list"? Or are you (also) enjoying the process?

If you are anything like me and love filling your plate with so many tasks that there is barely time to breathe, let alone give any of the activities you are doing the space and intention they deserve, this is a big ask. But if you want pleasure, the only way to access it is by slowing down and getting out of the habit of doing things just to get to the finish line. I have found that focusing on one thing at a time is the key to creating intention. For example, there is a massive difference between going out for a walk and replying to voice messages, answering emails and listening to podcasts while I'm walking, compared to when I go out for a walk without my phone and just enjoy the walk itself. If I focus on just the walk, I can add an intention for pleasure.

The second thing I mentioned is permission. Remember permission? Here it is again. This time in the context of pleasure, because even pleasure is something we need to give ourselves permission to experience.

Doing little things to add pleasure into your life *with intention* makes all the difference. You can call it a ritual if you like. I know many people who have rituals for the simplest of things – like running a bath, for example. The idea is not to do things automatically to get them done but rather do them slowly, with intent, and take pleasure in the detail.

I was thinking about how some innovations and technological advances, which are supposed to free up our time and give us more space for pleasure, might actually reduce our pleasure in the long run. I saw a video on social media about a robot that is supposed to be able to do your dishes and make you coffee and I couldn't help but think that if we end up having robots that can do everything for us, what will we actually do all day? People often assume pleasure means sipping a cocktail on a beach in Thailand, but there can be pleasure in brewing your own coffee, for example. There is pleasure in building stuff, in creating things. What I am trying to say is that I think there is pleasure in the process and if we are only focused on results and can't take any pleasure in the journey that gets us there, then what's the point? And I get it because we are taught to think in terms of efficiency. Things are done well if they are done fast and with minimal effort. But in my opinion that attitude is a pleasure killer. If we want to enhance pleasure in our lives then the focus has to shift from results to the process and the rhythm has to be slower.

What is holding you back?

Pleasure sounds amazing but many of us don't have a lot of it in our lives – which is strange, right? If it can be achieved easily by doing a variety of simple things, what's the problem?

I like what psychotherapist and broadcaster Esther Perel says about it in her book *Mating In Captivity*.[35] She explains that people sometimes wonder if we even deserve pleasure. If we are worthy of it. We have this idea that we can only have pleasure if and when we have paid for it in advance or will pay it back after – that pleasure for the sake of pleasure, without having to pay for it, is not okay, maybe even selfish.

And the word selfish is important here because, for a lot of people, the idea of taking time for themselves, engaging in their own pleasure, putting themselves at the top of the priority list is immediately associated with the idea of being selfish. Also, remember what we discussed earlier and how women in particular are taught to serve others and put other people's needs first before their own. When a woman takes time for herself, especially if she is a mother and this takes her away from her family, she is often perceived as selfish and is criticized/judged.

We also have created this idea of "fairness" in which pleasure is allowed but only in equal measures. People say "I work hard and I play hard", basically meaning that playing hard (i.e. having fun) is not allowed without working hard first. Again, we have to earn the right to our pleasure.

Why can't we just have fun without suffering or working hard (paying) for it first? Why is that not allowed?

You can also see this in relationships – the idea that one partner does not get more pleasure than the other. "How can I go out and leave my husband with the kids two nights in a row?" I've heard many women say this.

But what if we created what Esther Perel refers to as a "healthy sense of deserving" – i.e. knowing that it is okay to have pleasure even when your tasks are not done, even when you've just had a lot of it, even if your partner is carrying the load for you.

I know that to some of you that sounds like "selfishness", but it's not. Think about it – you have a right to feel pleasure, you deserve it not just because you've done something to earn it. That's the whole point of pleasure and that's what makes it so glorious.

Sacrifice

This was hard for me to accept – the mother in me, for example, truly believed that being a woman and mother meant *sacrifice*. Putting myself, my needs and my pleasure at the bottom of the priority list. This is what society tells us our job as a mother means, and I think many women struggle with this. Society constantly pushes mothers to this extreme – if you are not dishevelled by bedtime, shaking in a corner with a glass of Pinot, are you even a mother?

For me, taking time for myself, pursuing what gave me pleasure at the expense of time I could be dedicating toward my family, was the ultimate selfish act and something I found very hard to do.

Pushing back was a lengthy process and didn't happen overnight. It started with something as small and as simple as a 30-minute walk each day and evolved into much bigger chunks of time that I slowly but surely took for myself. I started taking pole dancing classes. At first just one class a week and at some point that grew to three classes. I took a girls' trip to Ibiza with a couple of friends and I even travelled all the way to Nepal with my brother for nearly three weeks to do the Everest Base Camp Trek. Then came a spa day with my girlfriends and spending two nights in a hotel attending a web summit in Lisbon (which is now an annual event). I love Ecstatic Dance workshops, where you dance for two hours straight with no alcohol and no speaking, connecting to your body and breathing plus Groove sessions and Secret Sunrises (dancing with headphones in nature). Regular treats are a good meal at a favourite restaurant and an excellent cocktail! And every time I imagined doing any one of those things for myself I was initially riddled with guilt and tormented with feeling selfish. I had to remind myself that I was a good mother and that doing things for myself and taking pleasure made me an even better one because the resentment and unhappiness I felt while my needs were not being met started fading away, and this was the best gift I could give my children. Again, I felt this responsibility to lead by example, demonstrating to my children my importance as an individual, apart from the "roles" I fulfilled. I want them to grow up seeing my independent needs being acknowledged and met.

Led by curiosity

I know that for some the idea of "pleasure" might feel too far from reach; it's like when people talk about having creativity in their lives, or passion – all of these concepts appear big and unachievable. I would even argue that these ideas can sometimes feel like added pressure – how many of you have been told to follow your passion or find your creativity, and felt unable to for fear that you might get it wrong? But I have found that if you follow your curiosity instead, you might actually stumble upon your passion, creativity and pleasure by accident. You see, while the other concepts can be broad, curiosity is easier to tackle. You have opportunities to be curious every single day, probably multiple times each day. Curiosity means asking "What is this?", following little paths that open up to you, embracing change and being interested in other people, saying "yes" to opportunities, asking questions, etc. Again, these are small simple "tweaks" that will have a subtle and noticeable effect on your energy, mood and outlook. There's nothing to lose.

SUGGESTION: IDENTIFYING PLEASURES

I invite you to look back at your list of needs and ask yourselves what would satisfy the need as pleasure? Because there can be pleasure in satisfying needs. For example, moving my hips could be satisfying as movement, yet if I took a second to put the music on, it becomes pleasurable. Let's try to complete the list with ways to find pleasure, and pay extra attention to where it feels difficult.

If it's easier, look for an area of your life in which you can introduce more pleasure. For movement, perhaps take up a dance class and move your body in a fun way that feels

FIND YOUR POWER THROUGH PLEASURE

good. What about going on a hike? Even something as small as stretching for ten minutes a day can feel pleasurable if you set pleasure as the intention, take your time and allow yourself to engage fully in it. A regular massage could be something you might enjoy – if you find body-to-body contact too intimate you can opt for alternatives that don't require taking your clothes off.

Take pleasure in preparing food or drink for yourself – can you find the time in your day/week to prepare a meal for yourself and really focus on pleasure? Rather than rush and eat whatever is there or drink your coffee cold, can you give yourself permission to brew your coffee, or cook your favourite dish from scratch and sit down for a meal and enjoy it? Again, think of the "ritual" of doing something special for yourself.

Other simple ideas might be:
- A hot bath with some candles and your favourite book
- A meditation session
- Visiting the gallery/exhibition of a favourite artist's work

LET'S TALK ABOUT
SEXUAL PLEASURE

The idea of being deserving of sexual pleasure, and taking charge of that, is extremely empowering and, of course, lots of fun. But unlike many other needs where lack of permission comes from feeling guilty and selfish, this particular area is more complex.

Firstly, most people don't even recognize it as a need. Pleasure in general, and sexual pleasure in particular, are perceived as a "luxury", something "extra", so noticing them feels way more selfish than attending to the basic needs for food, water, sleep, movement. Secondly, satisfying them is, more often than not, entangled with shame and body aversion and relationship dynamics, and hence more complex and not as straightforward as taking a walk.

Yet don't be mistaken – sexual pleasure is a very basic human need. Most of us need touch, physical pleasure, intimacy, physical release and, indeed, it could be as easy and straightforward to satisfy as any other physical need.

And it should be.

My second book, *You Did What?*, had a whole section dedicated to people's sexual confessions, which included a lot of talk about sexual needs not being met.[36] Some stories were about cheating and affairs and others more about the struggles of having this need that can't be expressed in a certain setting or relationship.

While the stories differed, what was clear from the amount of confessions sent in was the fact that sex and sexual pleasure is very much on people's minds, even if we don't discuss it openly enough. Sex, intimacy and self-pleasure are still somewhat taboo topics and linked to feelings of shame, or even trauma, and are not always easy to discuss. But sexuality, regardless of how hard or easy it is to talk about, is a massive part of being human and sexual pleasure needs to be viewed as one of our most basic needs.

In many cases it's a part of ourselves that can be shut down due to social norms, especially if you are female. The idea of women's desire existing has been denied and diminished throughout history. A woman's role in the sexual conversation has been non-existent – sex was deemed to be either about the satisfaction of men, or for making babies. The idea of women actually enjoying sex for enjoyment's sake, irrespective of the pleasure of their male partners, was not considered. Patriarchal societies throughout history have been obsessed with the female form and control over it, and the stigma against female pleasure and the female orgasm is part of that. In Victorian times "excess female desire" was deemed a cause of hysteria and insanity, with clitoris removal a potential remedy. We are still feeling the effects of science's historical inability to recognize the female orgasm outside of vaginal penetration, and the recognition of the importance and power of female masturbation is a modern idea.[37] Watch the TV series *Masters of Sex* for the story of female pleasure pioneers William Masters and Virginia Johnson in the 1960s.[38]

Let's talk about sex, baby

We don't talk about sex enough at all, particularly when we're first exploring the concept of sex and what it might mean. I know many parents find it hard to discuss with their kids, and when conversations do take place they are usually informative rather than anything else. And don't get me started on the way female genitalia have to have cutesy names rather than using the proper words. Many people have stories to tell about parental warnings about any sexual interactions. I was told sex was dangerous, that my virginity was something I ought to guard with my life, and that the sole goal of having sex was to have kids.

No one spoke of pleasure.

About 10–15 per cent of women haven't experienced an orgasm[39] but we don't talk about that. And when we do, it is often presented as something that is complicated and, generally speaking, an issue, a problem, a challenge (belonging to the woman, of course).

Even amongst friends, conversations about sex and self-pleasure can be sparse and awkward. I can tell you from my own experience as someone who is very open with her friends that not all of them feel comfortable talking about it. But community and gossip, in its positive sense, can play such a key role here.

Focusing on *our* needs and *our* pleasure while avoiding female competitiveness has the potential to empower us. Having these conversations makes the clear point that sex is important and that it's not selfish to focus on it. Talking openly with other women shifts something inside us. It reminds us that prioritizing pleasure, including sexual pleasure, isn't selfish or shameful but an essential part of being whole. By creating these safe, judgement-free spaces, we give each other the courage to own our needs unapologetically and to explore what brings us pleasure without guilt.

It's a topic many women would love to talk more about and I know this for a fact because so many women write to me every day and ask me to say more about it online.

Let's face it, if you are feeling shame or embarrassment about sex and sexual pleasure, if you feel that it takes special skills or knowledge, or if you are confused about it and think that it's not for you, then it is not surprising that it's something that you sideline, avoid or don't make a priority.

How can we get more pleasure into our lives, in its most sexual sense? How can we ignite that quality and awaken ourselves sexually? It is such a natural part of being human and, actually, sex and self-pleasure and orgasms are scientifically proven to help with our mental health and even our fitness.[40]

SUGGESTION: ENJOYING YOUR BODY

Take a few minutes with yourself to think of this question and come up with some ideas that actually fit with your life and the way you look at sex. Please try not to think about other people, as this makes things more tricky in many cases, but just about yourself – your body, your pleasure.

I want to suggest a few ideas of my own which you can ignore, or if you like them add them to your list and try them out:

- Oiling yourself after the shower or the bath and playing with your body.
- Standing naked in front of the mirror, noticing your body and the parts you especially like – there is a tendency to criticize ourselves, and compare to others, but try to focus on the parts you like and just let your body *be*.
- Surfing the net for some sex toys (not all are expensive and they come in many different prices for almost any pocket). If anyone needs any recommendations let me know because I honestly have them all.
- Full-on masturbation when you can – anyone who read my book *F*cked at 40* knows all about "mommy's special bath time". I am a particular fan of daytime solo loving ... (mainly because in the evenings I'm too tired).

SEXUAL PLEASURE

- A professional sensual massage is also a great way to get more in sync with the pleasure of touch on your body.

If you struggle to find ideas that appeal – ask yourself why? What's stopping you? It is always recommended to talk to a professional if you think you might need some extra help.

Often, I find it's just a need for the f*ck-it approach – finding the permission, and the acknowledgment that sex is a basic need.

Let's "gossip" about Mary...

She passed away in her 80s. She was frail and didn't weigh much when she took her final breath and I couldn't help but think about how sad it was that through her extraordinary life she never seemed happy with her body.

She had six children whom she raised nearly all by herself, because that was the way of the world at the time. Her husband worked long hours trying to create a better life than he'd had for his family, which meant she was often left alone to do it all — cook, clean, dress the kids, help with homework, take to the doctor, walk to school, etc. She did it all, sometimes with the help of her own mother and mother-in-law who, for periods of her life, lived with her in the same house.

She loved having them there with her and would smile whenever she spoke about that time when the house was filled with women of all ages having a natter, laughing and doing the housework and childcare together.

In their conversations they would, as women often do, complain about their bodies. "My hips are too big", "my breasts are saggy", "I don't like my big nose", "I wish I had a smaller stomach" are but a few examples she heard from her own mother and mother-in-law when she was a young wife. As the years went by, they became her own mantra which she repeated in front of her own daughters who later said the same things about their bodies in front of their own daughters.

She didn't mean to carry on this narrative — she barely realized this was a narrative that wasn't true, that had nothing to do with her and that she didn't have to subscribe to. All the women in her family before her did and she probably thought all the women who come after her will do too.

   I wish I could tell her that the cycle was broken.

CHAPTER EIGHT
FIND YOUR POWER THROUGH YOUR BODY

How does it make you feel to focus on your body? Where does your mind go? Do you think about what your body looks like, how it feels, how it moves or perhaps it's something else? How does how you feel about your body impact your life? Does it stop you from doing things? If you had to describe your body in a few words, what would those words be? Take a moment to think about that; you can also write the words down on a piece of paper. There is no right or wrong; it's just an observation so try not to judge what comes up.

As women we think a lot about our bodies. Not so much about how they feel or what they can do, but always what they look like – how we are physically seen. Our value, our self-worth, is often wrapped up with our exterior, so much so that at times it's hard to know what came first – feeling bad because of what we look like, or looking bad because of how we feel? Our bodies, with the help of some societal norms, regularly get in the way of our adventures, our needs, and our pleasure. Instead of being the main source of our pleasure – accepted, loved and celebrated – our bodies take, more often than not, the leading role as a barrier in our lives. For many they are a source of discomfort, shame or embarrassment and are hated, abused, neglected and even ignored.

Many of us feel like our bodies need to be fixed – we're conditioned from birth to feel ashamed of our appearance.

That something is wrong with us and that we need to change in order to be able to enjoy what we have. We tell ourselves we will wear the dress when we lose weight, or go to the beach in a bikini when we have more toned legs or arms, or go on a trek, ride a bike, take up pole dancing . . . whatever, when we feel happier about our bodies. That idea of having to "fix" something about our bodies before we can start doing something we love or think might be fun is rife. How many times have you said those types of things to yourself?

I used to say that to myself all the time.

"I really want to wear mini skirts but my knees are fat so I just need to lose some weight and then I will wear them."

"I've got a massive c-section shelf. I have to lose it and then I will go to the beach and wear a swimming costume."

"When I lose weight and have a flat stomach I will start tucking in my top."

"I have such hairy arms, I can't possibly wear short sleeve tops until I get rid of all my body hair!"

"I have small breasts, I can't wear a low-cut dress unless I get a boob job."

"I am too slim, I can't wear a tight-fitting t-shirt until I gain some weight and become curvier."

If any of the above sound familiar then please know that you're not alone. It's something we are trained to do from a very early age. The world around us is constantly suggesting ways to "improve" ourselves, especially when it comes to how we look – and especially as women. It is not surprising so many people are waiting to start their life when they can look different.

SUGGESTION: ACCEPTING YOUR BODY

Let's experiment with this for a minute. Take a minute to write down the last five times you thought about your body in an unaccepting way. Think about how much of your day is wasted around these thoughts and all of the things you don't do because of the way you don't accept your body.

For example, I don't go into the pool with my kids because I don't want to wear a swimming costume. I never show my hair in public because it is thin. I didn't join a dance class I really wanted to go to because everyone else had a smaller body than I do. I remember wasting hours of my day when I was calculating calories . . . stuff like that.

That is a little depressing, isn't it?

Try now to add a line to each of those time wasters and write down how your life might change if you didn't have those thoughts. How much time do you lose with this type of thinking? I want to start a positive process in which you think of all the nice things you could have been doing instead, had you not been obsessed, or even just occupied, with not accepting your body.

Please read your list with kind loving eyes and try to say "F*ck it" to the whole thing. How does that feel?

Judgement from ourselves

I started dating at the age of 14. I did all the diets, I was never happy with my weight even when I was very skinny, because at the end of the day it was never about my weight to begin with.

My size was never the issue. It was how I saw myself, how much I allowed myself to just *be*. How I judged myself.

You know, when I think of all the unkind things I've said to myself about my body it truly makes me sad. And also a little ungrateful. After all, this body had done so much for me, yet I took it for granted. It's something I could talk about for hours, but I'll just say that shifting the focus from what our bodies look like to what they do and how they function was fundamental for me.

Try making a list of all the wonderful things your body does for you and then look over that list when you have negative thoughts about it. Stuff like: my body gets me places, I can taste delicious food thanks to my body, my body makes beautiful babies, my body gives me pleasure, and so on . . . It is not how we are taught to think – we are taught to focus on looks (compared to an unnatural stereotype), but it's a matter of practice. The more you do it, the easier it will become.

It was only in my 40s when I truly said "F*ck it" about my body. Some things happen slowly and shifting my thinking from what my body looks like to what it does was a long process, but sometimes you have to jump in and hope for the best.

Remember learning how to swim, when you start with your floats and swim close to the edge, and then, at some point, you go to the deep end and you swim without aids. So for me with some things it was like that. I remember going to Italy on a family holiday and wearing a bikini for the first time in years. High-waisted, polka dot, super cute and extra large, and I just went for it. And the funniest thing about that experience was that I was literally expecting the sky to fall down on me or something. And I remember thinking after I had spent a whole day prancing around in that bikini, "Wow, nothing happened." The world did not end because of me in my bikini. The police did not show up. No one cared.

It suddenly felt not so dramatic.

Grab life

Trying little things is a good start – what would happen if you did wear that short skirt you always wanted to wear but didn't think you had the legs for? Can you walk around a whole day with your top tucked into your pants and survive? Why not go to a taster class of Zumba or pole dancing even if you're not a size 8?

I am a massive believer of exposure therapy and I have to say that the more I did the things I thought I could never do – big and small – and the more I practised saying "F*ck it", the easier it got.

And then there was also the realization that life is happening right now.

When I reached 40, I had a mid-life crisis, this realization that life is short and it's passing me by. I saw that all these things I was not letting myself do – because I was waiting to change something about my body – were things that I *could* do right now. The only thing stopping me was, in fact, *me*.

We have a choice about how to live our lives, but we do need to pay attention to ensuring that we don't allow society to restrict us. (And it's not just the body image stuff – even doing things like bungee jumping at 42, which is not what mothers/women are supposed to do, I had to overcome the idea that it might not be "right".) Of course there is immense pressure, especially when it comes to body image – the unrealistic beauty standards that are shoved down our throat everywhere, from movies and magazines to social media and the fashion industry. I get it, it's real. However, what is also real is that we *are* free to do what we want. We have a choice. No one can make us do what we don't want to do.

There is no actual law stopping us.

No one will arrest you if you go to the beach with your big thighs and cellulite. No one actually cares if you have body hair, or if your boobs are saggy. The world will continue if you flaunt what you've got or wear shorts that show your knees.

The police are not coming, you are free. For me this was a totally liberating concept.

I went from feeling restricted by external voices to realizing that ultimately I was restricting myself, and that I had the power to liberate myself. Sure, it might come with a price. People might stare, snigger or even make nasty comments, and that is scary and unpleasant. In fact I clearly remember when I was 15 walking home from a friend's house feeling pretty good about myself in my jeans and cropped top, when I heard a couple of boys say, "She's really pretty, such a shame about her body." And yes, I was crushed. At the time it felt like a massive blow and I wanted to lock myself in the bedroom and never come out again. But I wish I could go back to that day and tell my 15-year-old self that, 35 years later, as I am about to hit the big five-oh, I can't even remember what those two boys looked like! That's how insignificant they were in my life story. And that's how insignificant anyone who says anything about your body should be to you. It is your life, don't waste it on worrying about what other people think about what you look like.

Be free to just be

The "anti-aging" industry is immense, with tools like botox, fillers and procedures available to smooth you out and lift you up (physically). The "diet" industry is also mammoth as many women try every fad diet, shake or pill under the sun to lose weight. While I have no issue with women doing whatever they want to with their bodies, I do want to challenge the reasons as to why so many are trying to change what they look like.

Many women say that the self-grooming routine they do is for themselves, that they feel empowered by it and that it makes them feel good. But nearly all of us know that if we were living on a deserted island with no one else in sight, there is zero chance we'd shave our legs, change our eyebrows, colour our hair, do chemical peels, get boob jobs or cut out cake. The truth is that a lot of the things we do as women are done for the sake of fitting into a society that tells us women what we should look like. If wrinkles were celebrated in our world, would we spend so much money on anti-wrinkle products? If cellulite was considered pretty or normal, would we hide it? If tummy fat was labeled sexy, would we get tummy tucks? Most of the things we declare are "for ourselves" are, in reality, done for others.

We've convinced ourselves that we do it out of free will.

I'll own up and admit that I too 100 per cent take part in this culture – I remove body hair, I wear makeup, I colour my hair, I whiten my teeth, and I have tried numerous times to lose weight to have a certain body type that is more acceptable.

To set ourselves free from the restrictions of fashion, cultural norms and society's sexist attitude toward women is not an easy task but it is very much possible. This doesn't mean never wearing makeup again (I love a bold lip and no one will ever convince me to drop it). It doesn't mean we can't enjoy fashion or remove our body hair, but it does require a real look at why we do all the things we do to selectively decide which things we can maybe drop because actually they don't make us feel good about ourselves (and they are costing us a lot of money), compared to the things we enjoy doing that don't drain our time and resources.

Being slaves to fashion and the cosmetic industry is, of course, another way of keeping women poor and diminished and preoccupied with unimportant things. I read somewhere that the average American woman spends $225,000 in her lifetime on beauty products.[41] That's the price of an apartment or at least a downpayment on one! This statistic, alongside the fact that over 80 per cent of land in the world is owned by men, should be a wake-up call for all of us.[42] Even if these numbers are not accurate, because it's actually hard to know exactly how much we spend on these things and it also differs from country to country, I think it's at the very least safe to say that a lot of our time, energy and finances go towards maintaining or trying to achieve a certain look. Time, energy and money that could have maybe been directed elsewhere.

Historically, an attractive woman had a better chance of marrying – and for many women this was a necessary step because women didn't have financial independence and needed to be married – in today's world, women have more options. Rather than "marry well" women can (and are) making their own fortunes. It's still so ingrained in our culture that our looks are our biggest commodity, still supported by some men too, and we need to push back on this dumbing down of our power and attributes.

Feel the fear and do it anyway . . .

I know that for many of you the thought of stepping outside in an outfit you think suits only certain types of bodies is scary. I know that the fear is real and deep, and I know this because I have felt it with every fibre of my body. If anyone had told me a few years ago that I would post an unfiltered picture of my c-section shelf on social media *in profile*, I would have thrown up! But it's the small steps that we take, the little "F*ck it" moments that lead to the big ones, meaning you don't have to do it all at once. Start with something little and work your way up.

I asked a good friend to go shopping and choose outfits for me. She has a great sense of style and was always able to see something in me that I couldn't see. She would tell me how sexy I was when I felt frumpy and fat. And I wanted to see myself through her eyes. Whenever I would go shopping on my own I would always pick the same type of cut, the ones I thought "suited my body type" Because we are told to wear what suits our body type, right? Now in practice what this does is restrict us. It narrows the options and for me it made the experience of shopping really depressing. I would walk into a store and see all these great pieces of clothes and think, "I can't get any of those because they don't suit me/they're not right for someone with my body." I would end up buying something that looked a lot like everything else I had in my closet, and feeling very depressed about getting dressed.

I asked this friend to pick out outfits for me, and it was such an amazing experience. She chose things I would have never gone for! And for once it made the experience *fun*! Some things were terrible but a few items I love and I wear to this day! But that wasn't the point, which was to step out of that box I had placed myself in. Playing with this idea of what I was allowed to wear because of my body shape and just allowing myself to wear whatever I wanted.

What would happen if you did this too? Is there someone in your life you can go shopping with for a day? You don't even have to buy anything if you don't want to spend money, but just playing "dress-up" and seeing yourself through someone else's eyes will give you a fresh perspective and free your mind from the same old thinking.

The power to inspire others

They say that every time a woman shows up for herself, she shows up for all women, and I love this idea. That summer in Italy I was inspired by many other women I saw on the beach and around the swimming pool strutting their stuff at all ages and sizes. It made me feel good seeing other women free from inhibitions and judgement of their own bodies. Like a little boost of confidence that comes with numbers. When we see others allowing themselves to be free, we realize we can give ourselves permission too. I take inspiration from women who say, "The hell with that – wear what you want!" The inspiration isn't about the actual fashion choices, it's the fact that they don't care what other people are doing and/or saying about them. Just wear what you want.

This is where women communities and female friendships can really play a massive part. As women we spend a lot of our time and resources on talking and thinking about what our bodies look like. Imagine if, instead, we focused on lifting each other up. Personally, when my friends talk to me about their bodies I try not to engage in negative rhetoric. It's not about being insensitive to other people's insecurities or dismissing them, but I think that when we immerse ourselves in that type of bad talk about our bodies, we are doing ourselves and others a real disservice. There is enough of that from the outside world. It is up to us to encourage each other to change the narrative. If we hold each other accountable, in a supporting and loving manner, perhaps we can actually alter our perspective on the issue. I think we've been part of the conversation for so long, we don't even realize there are other options and it needs a collective effort to snap out of it.

Think about when your friends talk about the diets they are on – how do you react? I sometimes wonder if my own mother (who is 70 years old this year) will ever stop "watching her weight" or if one of my best friends in her mid-50s will ever stop reminiscing about the time she wore size 0 jeans when she was an 18 year old (which she still holds on to in case they ever fit again). We have to hold a mirror up to each other and say, "Girl, come on, you're fab, life is short, and we got bigger fish to fry!"

No regrets

People often tell me I am brave for prancing around in a swimming costume online and not giving a damn, but I don't see it as brave at all. It's the only body I have, you know – what other body am I supposed to prance around in?! Am I supposed to borrow someone else's for the day? No. This is it. But beyond that, I always say that the thought of when I am gone motivates me to live fully now: I often wonder what people will say about me when I am dead and I am pretty sure they won't be talking about my size or my wrinkles. Just like I am sure, without even knowing you, that the most uninteresting thing about you is what you look like. Yet think about how much time we dedicate to our appearance! It's crazy, right?

But I also know that my last dying thought, when I am 120 years old on my deathbed, will not be about my weight, and the reason I know this is because I did almost die once. About 12 hours after the twins were born I went into eclampsia (which means my body was poisoning itself) and I was seizing, my blood pressure was going crazy and the likeliest outcome was coma at the very best and possibly death. So as I was shaking on a hospital bed with my body completely out of control, alarm bells were ringing and doctors rushing in, with drugs being pumped into my veins left, right and centre. And I was just thinking, "Ohhhhhh, this is it, I am about to die; this is the moment", and waiting for the white light everyone talks about. Yet all I could think about was how amazing it feels to snowboard in white powder, and how delicious my favourite chocolate tastes, and how the best smell in the world was my babies' hair. I could smell it!

And then I saw my husband Mike sitting in the corner of the room looking so confused, and I realized he had no idea that I was about to die, and I remembered how he doesn't even know how to tie up our daughter's hair, and I thought "I can't die!" So I decided to live. And eventually my blood pressure came down and I was fine, but the point is that in all that time never once did I think, "Wow, I wish I'd eaten more kale and less cake when I had the chance!" My looks, my body size, the number of calories I consumed – none of that crossed my mind. The only things I thought about were the things that gave me *pleasure*.

Remember pleasure? That's all there was at the very end.

The things that make you happy and bring you joy are the only things worth worrying about, everything else is just noise.

SUGGESTION: CHANGING THE WAY YOU SEE YOURSELF

Think about one little thing you can experiment with? Is it tucking your top in for the day or having your hair down for the day? Maybe wearing a different style of skirt or jeans that you really like, or a brighter colour that makes you stand out? What would happen if you gave it a go? How would you feel if you did it for a whole day and survived? Write down a challenge and see if you can do it. Note how it made you feel.

Also, consider the inner dialogue you have with yourself about your body. This is like a conversation between your head and your body. What does your head say about your body? How does it talk to it and about it? Is it kind and accepting or judgemental and negative?

To give you an example, my head might say stuff like this:

"I hate you."

"I look at you and I feel shame."

"Why are you not good enough?"

It could also say:

"Thank you for doing a hard job, I know I am not always kind to you but you have been there for me and for that I am grateful."

"Sorry for abusing you."

"I want to love you."

Etc.

Then turn the tables and talk to your head as your body. What does your body feel? What does it have to say to your head in response or just generally speaking?

The conversation might look like this:

"Why are you so mean to me? I am trying my best."

"I wish you didn't say so many horrible things about me, it really hurts my feelings."

> It might be something like this:
> "Thank you for looking after me."
> "Hey, lets go have fun this summer, I am ready to rock that bikini if you are!"
>
> This is a VERY powerful exercise, one I suggest you do repeatedly.
>
> The point is not to be negative or positive here. The point is to listen and notice what this inner dialogue sounds like. It might surprise you to hear what your body has to say and it might make you feel more compassion for it. When I did this exercise, that is what I experienced. Other people have other experiences and there is no right or wrong, good or bad. It's an opportunity to listen.

Women have so much more to offer the world than our looks and the more we spend time together, connecting, encouraging one another, teaching, learning, building, investing and being authentic, the less time we will have to worry about what other people think about the veins in our legs or the shape of our upper lip.

Enjoy your bodies and don't let them stop you embracing life in all its glory.

Let's "gossip" about Elinor...

Of all my friends, Elinor is the one that truly has it all together. Not because she can juggle a million things all at once like a ninja, but rather because she doesn't.

Most of my friends are involved in so many different things — they work, they are mothers, they volunteer at school, do yoga, do charity, host parties, cook from scratch, care for elderly parents, have tidy homes and get their nails done once every three weeks.

Not Elinor though.

A few years ago I discovered how she is always so calm. We were both spending the afternoon at another friend's house and the other friend and I were ranting about how hectic life was and how tired we were. Elinor listened to the conversation while sipping her tea and smiled. After a few minutes I asked how she was doing and if she could relate. She said, "To be honest, Tova, I can't relate but that's probably because I don't do as much as you do. I don't volunteer at the kids' school, the kids only have one after-school activity and it's at the school on the same day, they have fish fingers and baked beans for dinner at least three times a week, and we don't host very often so my house looks like a hurricane just hit it!"

She continued: "I know that some people might see me as lazy or like I am not doing enough, that my life is far from perfect because the kids are bored most Sundays because we don't do much and the house is a tip — but I don't care. I have time to see my friends, do my walks, read books, sip tea while it's still hot ... and for me that's a win, that's perfection. I don't want to do more, I just wanna be happy, and doing less makes me happy."

Mind blown!

CHAPTER NINE
FINDING YOUR POWER THROUGH DOING LESS

Are you constantly exhausted? Do you reach the end of the day feeling like you've barely survived, never mind managed to do all the things you were supposed to do? Does your "to-do list" never seem to get shorter? Do you wake up on Monday morning feeling like it should be Friday? If you've answered yes to these questions, you probably need to do less! How does that thought make you feel? Does it make you feel anxious and worried ("But who will do it all if I am doing less?"), or does it make you feel excited ("Sign me up now" type of thing)? Try to imagine what your life would look like if you did less. Is there one particular area in your life in which you might be doing too much or is it just a general theme? Take some time to think about these things and you can write down your thoughts and reflect on them if you wish.

I feel that the subject of making time/space in order to find yourself has come up already many times in these chapters. Between work, any kids or dependents or aging parents, running the household and our social lives, life can get pretty hectic. Our brains are like supercharged computers, running multiple programs all at once, constantly jumping between work, family, to-do lists, and even the occasional Ryan Gosling fantasy (because, hey, we need balance). Be honest, have you ever seen a woman do just *one* thing at a time? I'm pretty sure this is why they invented the hands-free vibrator – so that we can multitask even while having an orgasm!

If I had to make a list of all the roles I "hold", it would look a little bit like this: chef, chauffeur, cleaner, tutor, meal planner, stylist, butt wiper, sock hunter, shoe tracker, spoon locator (basically, private detective), event planner, personal assistant, snack provider, referee, coach, teacher, storyteller, travel agent, therapist, Head of HR, marketing manager, CEO, COO, CFO, production manager, stunt double, ninja warrior, monster slayer, Santa Claus, the Easter Bunny, and the goddamn Tooth Fairy.

In short, my LinkedIn bio simply says: "FUCKING EXHAUSTED".

Welcome to the "mental load", where managing the home, keeping track of appointments, planning meals, booking holidays, remembering birthdays and generally solving problems before they even exist is like running a company. And we're supposed to make sure all this is done while having great hair and time for an elaborate skin routine.

And before anyone wonders about my husband Mike, I'll have you know he does it all too. From the cooking to the school run and helping with homework, there is nothing my husband doesn't do, and the only reason I remember this so clearly is, of course, because he always tells me. "Darling, I'm taking out the bins", "Darling, I'm cooking dinner", "Darling, I'm taking the dogs out" . . . you get the idea. But you see, the mental load isn't just the "doing" of the tasks, it's the planning. It's seeing the full picture in 3D and anticipating things that haven't even happened (and may never happen) ahead of everyone else. It's like being a PA, event manager and fortune teller all at the same time.

And this mental load is rarely acknowledged. It is the invisible work of women that doesn't get recognition. All those little tasks women do that others seem to think are done by themselves. From picking up things off the floor and putting items back where they belong to filling water bottles and changing toilet rolls, asking about donations for school events and costume requirements, buying party presents and arranging playdates, booking babysitters and speed-washing favourite t-shirts, and so on. These are the little and big tasks that we do each day that individually don't seem like much but when you add them all up they weigh heavy on our shoulders and are felt by women everywhere. Even in households where both partners work and where tasks are shared, women are often the ones expected to carry the invisible burden of *thinking* about what needs to be done and doing just that little bit more.

And the truth is, women excel at it. Not because we are biologically designed to, but because society has conditioned us to manage it all and solve problems before they exist. I could be cooking dinner while also mentally solving world hunger, chatting on the phone with a friend who is going through a breakup while closing all the drawers in our kitchen with my butt and combing my daughter's hair with my foot. The amount of things I manage to do all at once is outstanding but it also doesn't seem to impress anyone because half of the population are experts at it too.

Remember that term "you can have it all"? It is attributed to Helen Gurley Brown, editor of *Cosmopolitan Magazine* and author of the 1982 book *Having it All: Love, Success, Sex, Money, Even If You're Starting with Nothing.* Her book was a guide for women to achieve both professional success and personal happiness, encouraging them to strive for success in both departments. This idea resonated deeply during the 1980s, a time when women were entering the workforce in larger numbers and cultural shifts around gender roles were accelerating.[43]

However, the concept of "having it all" evolved into a broader discussion around work–life balance (for women) and it came to symbolize the sometimes unrealistic expectation that women could successfully manage both a high-powered career and family life, without having to compromise in either area.

I believe that the main reason this concept became unrealistic is because it was mistakenly thought that *having* it all meant *doing* it all.

Show me a man that *does* it all.

Most men who are considered to "have it all" usually have a wife. They are not expected to *do it all* – they are allowed to focus on one thing at a time while someone else makes sure all the other stuff gets done. But women, on the other hand, rarely enjoy the same privilege. Women who want to have it all are expected to *do it all* too, possibly as a punishment for daring to want it all in the first place. And this consent to doing it all is, I agree, very much unrealistic. It is why so many women are burned out.

But can anyone blame us for trying to do it all, though? For too long, women were left behind, having to fight for a seat at the table, which eventually came (reluctantly) with a condition – if you want to be here you're gonna have to work twice as hard as anyone else.

And that's what we do. Work twice as hard as anyone else, sometimes at the expense of our own health and sanity. And while the reasons are clear to me, I also know that it's unsustainable in the long run and, more importantly, it's not empowering. Female empowerment isn't just about breaking glass ceilings – it's about sharing the load, being able to take a break and not feel guilty about it, and also about letting go of perfection. Because sometimes, the greatest act of empowerment is simply doing *less*.

I briefly touched on this in the earlier chapter about wisdom. But before I continue, I would like to tell you that the thought of doing nothing or doing less used to petrify me. Who would I be if I didn't have 20,000 plates spinning in the air all at once? How can I not do my absolute best 100 per cent of the time? And on a more practical note – how will things get done if I am not planning them and making sure they get done?

Establishing the distribution of chores

For many couples, household chores are a major source of conflict. Who does what, who does more, whether things are done the "right" way or fast enough – these are common arguments. Most couples I know don't have an equal split when it comes to household responsibilities, and it's usually the woman who ends up carrying more of the load. There are various reasons for this. For some, the reasoning is that if one partner (usually the man) earns more, then the woman should take on more of the housework. But we all know that this logic doesn't hold up. Household tasks never end; there's no clocking out, no weekends off, no holidays. It's a 24/7 job, and you just can't compare that to any other full-time position.

My husband and I share the household chores pretty equally. But it wasn't always like this. For years I carried more of the load than he did, despite having a job and equally contributing to our finances. How this happened isn't clear to me. I guess we just fell into these roles without much intention; I just did things and somehow they became my job. And then one day, as I "dropped the ball" and forgot an important school-related task because I had too many things to think about, I turned to my husband and asked why he wasn't on our kids' class WhatsApp groups and he said, "I don't know." And it hit me that there were so many things he wasn't doing for no particular reason. So I added him to the class WhatsApp groups and it marked a turning point in our relationship and how we would share the responsibilities between us.

I have this theory that in every relationship, there's a small window at the beginning where the distribution of household jobs is established, and the secret is to *resist the urge to do it all yourself*! Yes, I know you can probably do it better and faster, but the key to long-term sanity is to let your partner figure it out. It's like a standoff: who can tolerate the mess longer? Who will break first? It's a battle of wills that can determine who ends up taking on which responsibilities, possibly for the rest of your relationship.

Trust me, I know how hard it is. You'll watch your partner who's taken out the clothes from the washing machine and is about to hang them, but he didn't shake the clothes before hanging them – and you know that if he doesn't shake them they will take five years to dry and will be creased and horrible when they eventually do. Your eye will start to twitch, your palms will get sweaty and you'll want to jump in and scream, "Just shake it!" *and offer to do it yourself.*

DON'T*!*

Yes, it may never be to your standard and you may need to compromise. My sheets, for example, have been creased since 2006, and you know what, I'm okay with it.

"Busy" isn't always a good thing

How many times have you been asked by a friend, "How are you?" and you have replied, "Busy"? I do it all the time and it's something I'm really working on. Busyness has become a state of mind and it's really a big old obstacle to finding your power. In fact, I would argue that constantly "being busy" is a power-sucker because it takes over everything. In that state of mind there is no room for prioritizing your needs. There is no focus on pleasure. There is no playfulness and no space for wisdom.

Our whole culture is based on filling up every single minute of the day with "doing something". It's even become rare to see children doing nothing. Kids' schedules these days are almost as busy as adults', filled with art lessons, after-school sport activities, playdates, birthday parties, music or dance practice, etc, with zero down-time to just chill, stare at the wall and do absolutely nothing. While we and generations before us were allowed to be bored, kids today never have a dull moment and many parents seem to encourage this. Whether it's because they want to make sure their kids get the best education and a headstart in life and they think smart kids don't just read magazines or play in the mud, or whether it's because they prefer their kids to "do something" rather than scroll endlessly on their phones – the result is the same.

We are raising a generation of children that are doing way too much and will grow up to be adults who do way too much.

There is a really sad moment in Winnie-the-Pooh that comes to mind, where Christopher Robin says he won't be able to do "nothing" anymore and Pooh asks him why. Christopher Robin's reply is: "They don't let you."

We don't let our kids do "nothing", just like we don't let ourselves do "nothing" either. We fill our days with more and more tasks, often to distract ourselves from focusing on other things and sometimes because we feel guilty to (god forbid) do less. It is also related to our fear of being bored. What will we find in those moments of nothing when we have the space to look inward rather than be distracted by the constant noise?

The burnout of the constant state of "busy" is felt by all, especially women, and doing less is the key to breaking this cycle that sets you up for failure.

Doing less

What would happen if you did less? I can imagine most of you think this is an impossible task and perhaps your greatest worry is: "But who will do all the things that need to be done if I don't?"

I would like to explore a few ideas here: firstly, are you expecting too much of yourself? Meaning, while there are obviously a lot of things that need to be done around the house, at work, with the kids, etc, have you set the bar very high for yourself? Do you aim for perfection or are you happy to settle for "good enough"?

I remember reading years ago about the "Good Enough Mother" theory which was coined by the British pediatrician and psychoanalyst Donald Winnicott in his famous book *Playing and Reality*.[44] It profoundly changed the level of pressure I put myself under when it came to motherhood. If at first I was aiming for "best mother of the year award", I basically lowered my standard and set it at "good enough", which meant I wasn't so hard on myself when things didn't go as planned. I didn't have to be perfect. I didn't have to kill myself trying to be the best mother there ever was.

This took so much pressure off and allowed me to "do less". I was still able to aim high in some areas that I wanted to, but I didn't have to aim high all the time and with everything. I got to choose.

I have applied this theory to other aspects of my life and at times where I feel pressured to be "the best", I ask myself if being "good enough" instead is also acceptable. Sometimes the answer is "no", so I try harder. But many times the answer is "yes", so I let myself off the hook and instead of doing 100 per cent I do 80 per cent or even less. I understand that this goes against the idea of always doing your best and trying your hardest – we tell our kids to do this with their school work and sports, and we even commend them for it, rather than focus on their results. But you always have to weigh it against the price you pay for aiming your highest. If you're fine and it's not taking a toll, that's great! But if you find that aiming for 100 per cent is causing you to feel stressed, tired, resentful or unhappy, if it's impacting your health, or if it means you have no room and time for resting, playing and attending to your needs, then think about lowering the bar as a first step toward allowing yourself to *do less*.

The second thing I want you to do is to challenge the idea that if things don't get done by you, they simply will not get done at all. I used to think that if I didn't do everything all the time for everyone else, then nothing in my house would ever get done. This included housework, cooking, making appointments, booking holidays, walking the dogs and so on. I also found that trying to motivate my husband and children to do things instead of me always doing them didn't always work. They would take on some of the tasks but very quickly would stop and I would find myself in the driver's seat again.

However, what did help was when I just started doing less.

It didn't happen overnight, but as time went on, the fact that I stepped back in some areas made space for others to take charge more. It's not easy doing this, especially if you're anything like me and you like things to get done fast and in a certain way, but it does work. To be honest this works not just with housework, it works with relationships too. When you change, the people around you change too. Everything in life is a balancing act and if you change one thing in a system that has multiple parts, everything else in that system has to adjust accordingly.

The point I am trying to make is that you will never know what will happen if you do less unless you try it.

Asking for help and leaning on your community

Why not challenge the idea of having to do it all by yourself? Asking for help is the key to doing less. Why do it alone if you can do it with others? Who said you had to do it all by yourself in the first place? We are so afraid of telling other people we need their help because we think it means we have somehow failed, but possibly the best-kept secret is in fact that we would all love to be able to lean on others more often and maybe if we allowed ourself that (even if it starts as "gossip") then perhaps we will all be better for it?!

For me this has always been the key to female power. The idea of leaning on other women, asking for help when needed and having a support system rather than doing it all by yourself. When I became a mother the need for other women's support became very obvious to me, and the absence of it was at times harder than the new parenting challenges themselves. At the time, I was living far from my own mother and sister and most of my friends hadn't had children yet and I felt very alone. Sure, I had my husband and he tried his best to be supportive. But as much as he tried, there simply is no replacement for female companionship.

I needed someone to say, "Let me have her, you go have a shower, I'm also going to clean your kitchen and make you a cup of tea and when you're ready, if you want, I'll paint your nails bright pink just for fun. I also have some juicy gossip to tell you about that hot neighbour of mine. But if you prefer we can just sit here and watch *The Holiday* in silence and eat chocolate." I love my husband, but there is no universe in which he will ever know to say any of that stuff and to be fair to him, I wouldn't want him to. It's the type of thing you want to hear from your girlfriends.

You see, we need women around us to lift us up when we are low, and to high five us when we are on top. We need women to be our mirrors, to reflect back to us that we can do hard things and that we are capable and strong. We need women to say it's okay not to have it all together at all times. We need a support system to lean on and we need to give ourselves permission to ask for help and receive it when it is offered to us.

When I had my first child I felt embarrassed to ask for help, or even admit that I couldn't do it by myself. Somewhere along the way I had learnt that this was not allowed. But in fact, women's communities are built on the idea of being a big village, where everyone helps with each other's kids, and no one is expected to do everything alone or in isolation.

I started my blog back in 2015 and most of the members of my online community were indeed mothers. Many of them wrote in to tell me how lonely they were feeling. For a lot of them, female friendships were something they simply never had and it amazes me every time I discover how many women still feel this sense of isolation. Not only because of geographical restrictions, but also because they can't imagine a world where women help each other out.

FINDING YOUR POWER THROUGH DOING LESS

So many women simply do not trust other women, so how could they ever ask another woman for help? But asking for help is key. Being vulnerable enough to admit when you simply can't do it all by yourself means giving yourself permission to be true to yourself, which is at the heart of finding your power.

And I'll tell you another secret – it doesn't even have to be a result of not being able to do it all. You can just choose not to do it, even if you can. Meaning, don't wait until you're totally burnt out and running on empty or have hit the wall to fill up your cup. Just because you are capable of doing it all by yourself doesn't mean you have to. You can fill up your cup even if there's still some left in it. I realized this some years ago after I had reached my tipping point on several occasions and actually fell ill before I allowed myself to take time off. It was as if my body was sending me a clear signal saying, "Girl, you gotta rest." I didn't listen and I carried on, even when I knew I had taken on too much, and eventually I got sick and was forced to stay in bed for a few days and rest. This happens to a lot of women – we can just do less for no reason and not feel guilty about it. It's okay.

SUGGESTION: LOOK FOR TIME SAVERS

See if you can identify areas in your life in which you can do less/show up less. This doesn't have to mean not doing them at all, although if there are things you can completely drop then that's great, but it can be as simple as just lowering the bar. For example, if you like volunteering at your kids' school but it's also super stressful and very time-consuming, see if you can reduce your involvement. Could you only do one bake sale rather than five of them, for example? Or help on the day but be clear that you're not available for set-up and clear-up.

Think about what you do when you have free time on your hands – do you immediately add things to your calendar because you can't stand the thought of having free time, or could you try enjoying the space you have? How can you outsource your responsibilities rather than have to do them all yourself – are there friends or family you can lean on? Perhaps you are in a position to pay for help, in which case what's stopping you from doing that?

Make a list of some things that are most time consuming and see how you can improve those specific areas. As always, start with small changes and see how they feel. If you are a high achiever in most areas of your life and perform at a high standard, ask yourself who has put this pressure on you – do you feel others expect perfection from you or could it be that this is a pressure you've placed on yourself? Imagine what would happen if you did less – what price would you actually pay vs what you would gain?

SUGGESTION: LIST YOUR CURRENT COMMITMENTS

Draw up a list of your recurring tasks, responsibilities and obligations and break them into categories (work, household, self-care, kids, social obligations, etc). Then rank them in terms of importance, but make sure to take into account how essential they are in bringing you joy or value? Are they essential to your goals and also well-being? And finally ask yourself if someone else could do them instead of you?

This simple practice helps you to identify what you can drop or delegate. Once you have created some space in your schedule, make sure you block it in your diary so you don't fill it back up with other tasks! It's important to also go back to review how doing less is impacting your life and to adjust the approach as needed.

LET'S TALK ABOUT
SETTING BOUNDARIES

What pops into your head when you hear the word "boundaries"? Is setting boundaries something you find easy to do? Do you even know what boundaries are? Do you have any in place? How does it feel when you encounter someone else's boundary? Do you find saying "no" easy or is it really hard? Do you feel rejected when someone else says "no" to you? Take a few moments to think about these themes, and write down what pops up for you.

Boundaries are not an area of expertise for me, but from my experience I have learnt they are so important. The way I see it, absolutely key to doing less and finding time and space in your life to explore all of the ideas in this book is the issue of boundaries, and why we are *so* bad at putting them in place for ourselves – for our emotional health as much as to reduce the unfeasible demands of life. So many women I know find it near impossible to say "no". It makes them feel mean, ungenerous and even selfish.

As women we are brought up to please others. We are conditioned to be nice, polite and put everyone's needs ahead of our own, so it's no surprise that many of us struggle to prioritize our own needs and just say "no". I don't think I was aware of the concept of "boundaries" till my 30s. It's just not something anyone ever explained to me. I was not taught to protect my energy. Instead I was taught to care for others even if it meant my own needs were at the bottom of the priority list.

When I was little I was a "people pleaser". I would often look to people to take their cue as to how I was supposed to behave or even what I was meant to say. I didn't look inward because I didn't realize that I had an inner voice in the first place. Permission was always something I looked for from others. That's why it's no surprise that I also struggled to say "no".

What are boundaries?

The way I see it, boundaries are limits we set for ourselves to protect ourselves. It can be something physical, verbal or even emotional, and is basically a sort of guideline to what we find unacceptable behaviour toward us. Boundaries are about who we give power to in terms of deciding for us how we live our lives.

I know that a lot of women feel like it's their job to manage other people's lives and emotions. We tell ourselves this story – that if we don't do this, everyone will fall apart. I am guilty of this too. I remember when my parents separated in my early 20s, my little sister was only a teenager and was still living at home. She was very upset by the breakup and I for whatever reason took it upon myself to deal with her grief rather than deal with my own. I wanted to be a good big sister, so I put how I was feeling about the breakup aside and focused on helping her get through it. I had this idea that I had to manage it all, even if it meant completely neglecting myself. Six months down the line I started getting panic attacks and began therapy.

What I was lacking were boundaries. A protective border that kept me safe from giving too much. I felt that if I said I couldn't be there for her at the level she needed, it made me selfish and a bad person. But really, being able to say that I had nothing left to give would not have been an act *against her* but rather an act of self-preservation. I see that now, but at the time I didn't.

I can see a similar pattern with how I approached motherhood. When the kids were little I was determined to do anything in my power to ensure their happiness and desperately tried to manage their emotions while at the same time ignoring my own. As they grew older it became very clear to me that there would be a lot of things I couldn't fix and the best gift I could give them was to teach them to manage their own emotions.

Trying to manage other people's emotions is not only exhausting, it's also totally impossible. It's also not your job to manage other people's emotions. Your job is to manage your own emotions. And this doesn't mean you stop caring and loving the people in your life. You can absolutely carry on being supportive and try to help when you can, but you do not have to take on their emotional well-being. It's not our job, and if it feels like it is, consider the possibility that this is a story you have chosen to tell yourself. You have the power to tell yourself a different story, in which *your* emotions also matter.

We also have to be able to release ourselves from this idea that we need to please others. One of the things that really helped me let go of my need to please people and my constant worry about letting others down or disappointing them was the book *The Let Them Theory* by Mel Robbins. In the book she talks about putting yourself first and not taking on the responsibility for other people's happiness. It's natural we would want to please others but in doing so we let ourselves down and compromise our own happiness. The idea is that it's not your responsibility and that you should just *let them* feel and react in any way they want because you're not responsible for other people's emotions. It's *their* job.

"No" is a full sentence

"No" is a full sentence and doesn't need explaining. It's your right to say "no" and it does not make you a bad person, or a mean person, or a selfish person.

Of course, boundaries are so much more than just saying "no". While saying "no" is definitely a key part, boundaries are more about expressing what feels right for you. For example, physical boundaries are about personal space and what you feel comfortable with in terms of touch. Emotional boundaries remind you that you don't have to take on other people's emotions as your own. Mental boundaries give you the freedom to hold your own beliefs without feeling pressured to agree with others. And time boundaries are about knowing how much of yourself you can give to others while keeping some energy and time for your own needs. You can set boundaries in different places in your life; it's about being clear on your red lines and what you will not tolerate.

A lot of women I know struggle to set boundaries. This is because women are often socially and culturally conditioned to prioritize the needs of others, often at the expense of their own. Many identify as caregivers, feeling an inherent responsibility for others' emotions and well-being, and internalize the belief that they must never disappoint or fail to meet others' expectations. This dynamic often includes cultural pressures to always be nice, avoid expressing anger in healthy ways, and take on the stress of others, which can have tangible effects on mental health and even the immune system. These patterns are deeply ingrained, making it challenging for women to set boundaries or prioritize self-care, perpetuating cycles of stress and emotional exhaustion.

Setting boundaries is your way of saying, "This works for me, and this doesn't."

"No" is not a rejection

Setting boundaries is not about keeping people out – it's also about letting the right things in, on your terms.

I think it's important to understand this because it can also help you cope when someone else says "no" to you. It's easy to take a "no" as rejection. I've seen this happen a lot, especially with women, because we are very fast to look for the fault in ourselves when people turn us down. But another way to reinterpret the "no" we get from others is that it is simply them expressing *their* boundary. Looking at it this way helped me shift how I reacted to their (negative) answer.

The "no" was no longer about me but rather about them.

Most people perceive "no" as a rejection and this can feel very painful. But when you reframe the "no", you receive from others and see it as an expression of their boundary, rather than as a rejection, it takes the focus off you. In fact, in most cases people's boundaries will have nothing to do with you. Most times people say "no" for reasons that have nothing to do with the person they are saying no to. But as women in particular we are quick to assume it's personal or that we've done something wrong. Reminding yourself that when someone says "no" is simply them expressing their boundary will help you cope with their answer.

You might be disappointed, but you don't need to feel rejected.

Boundaries create a safe space

When I began running my retreats, it became clear right away that boundaries were going to be a recurring theme. But instead of spending days just talking about them, I found that actually practising boundaries was much more impactful. During the first group circle, I emphasized that no one should feel obligated to say or do anything they weren't comfortable with. I also encouraged everyone to express their boundaries openly, because that's how we create a safe space. In fact, real safety in any group and in friendships comes from knowing that everyone feels free to communicate when something doesn't work for them. If I can trust that someone will tell me when their boundary has been crossed, I can relax and be more open with them. Otherwise, I'd constantly worry about unintentionally upsetting or hurting them, and that hesitation can block real connection.

What I am trying to say is that boundaries aren't just about protecting ourselves – they're also a gift we give others. By sharing our limits, we're giving people a roadmap to avoid unintentionally causing harm. It's like a public service for healthy relationships! Setting boundaries helps everyone feel safer, and that's the foundation for real honesty and vulnerability.

Roleplaying with boundaries

Practising boundary-setting is essential if you find saying "no" difficult. I suggest starting with small things and always focusing on yourself rather than on other people's behaviours:

"I don't feel comfortable with . . ."
"XX doesn't work for me . . ."
"I'm not able to commit . . ."

Framing it this way rather than using "stop saying/doing this" usually goes down better when people are presented with our boundaries. Practising saying the actual word "no" can be helpful too, though, to be very clear on the message. "No" is not a terrible word when delivered firmly and clearly without emotion. Learning how to cope when someone else says "no" to us is equally important.

Why not rope in a trusted friend to role play with you as practice – getting them to ask you to do things for them and you practising saying "no" (even if yes seems reasonable). For example, they might ask you to make them a cup of tea, or give them a hug, stroke their hair, tell them a joke . . . it can literally be anything, big or small, and no matter what they say, you have to say "no". The trick is to do this clearly and confidently without explaining why, or apologizing.

It's okay to say "no". You don't have to feel guilty, it's your right, and the more you practise, the easier it gets. The same works in reverse – ask your trusted friend to do certain things, such as help you with a simple job, and no matter what you ask, they have to say "no". See if you can remind yourself when they reject your request that they are not rejecting you, but rather expressing their own boundary. Can you cope with their "no" without it devastating you? The more you practise this in a safe space, the easier it will be to cope with it when it happens in real life. Of course if there are people in your life who disrespect your boundaries repeatedly and cause you harm, distancing yourself from them and relevant situations might be the best course of action. It all depends on who they are and what the boundary is.

SUGGESTION: KNOWING YOUR OWN BOUNDARY NEEDS

Create two lists: on one list, you write situations where you struggle to say "no" (for example, accepting extra work or staying late at an event), and on the other, you list situations where you feel comfortable asserting a boundary or saying "no". You then visualize scenarios for each situation on the first list, imagining someone asking you to do the task or favour. Practise responding assertively but kindly with a "no" that explains your boundary. For example: "I appreciate you asking, but I can't take on more work right now" or "I need to prioritize my own time, so I'll have to decline. Thank you for the invitation." Again, it will help to role-play with a trusted friend but you can also do this in front of the mirror. After practising, take note of your feelings. Did saying "no" make you uncomfortable? What language felt more natural? You can then adjust your approach based on what works best for you. This should enable you to gently start implementing it in real life. Remember to use "I" statements to express your needs rather than blame others. It's okay to be firm while staying respectful and be careful to avoid over-explaining – it's a good thing to have boundaries!

Let's "gossip" about Laura...

It's 10pm on a Tuesday. I'm usually in bed by 9 but instead I am walking the streets of Lisbon with Laura and Amy looking at Christmas lights after having an amazing meal and three cocktails. It's Laura's "going away party". She and her family are moving back to the US after two and a half years and we wanted to do something fun to mark the occasion before she leaves.

I'm gutted to see her go.

We met in August 2022, a few weeks after we had landed in Portugal. I posted an ad on Facebook saying we're new in the area and asking if anyone would be interested in meeting up at the beach. Laura replied. Our kids are the same ages so we met up that afternoon and immediately hit it off.

We became friends and she has been such a big part of my experience here — we've travelled together, had brunches on her terrace, seen each other through family and health struggles, and laughed together so much... and honestly, I can't picture life here without her.

At dinner Amy and I gave her a bracelet we got her as a going away gift. It had a shamrock on it for good luck. Laura got teary and we held hands.

We left the restaurant and on the way to the car we took a few photos in front of the lights and joked about how silly it was to wear heels out. As we were about to head home Laura turned to us both and said: "I wish we had done this even more. Of all the things I am going to miss in Portugal, our friendship is what I will miss most."

I will miss her so much.

CHAPTER TEN
CALL UP THE GIRLS

I hope that all the suggestions, stories and ideas I've shared with you will help you find your power. Whether it's through focusing on your needs, or finding pleasure even in the little things (and working it more and more into your life), listening to your inner voice and your own wisdom, trying to incorporate playfulness into your routine, setting boundaries, doing less, gossiping, letting go of shame or possibly through the most important thing of all – your relationships with other women. The point is that your female power is in reach – you just need to grab it.

Be unapologetic

One day a few years ago I walked into a door and automatically said "sorry". Yes, I apologized to a *door* for walking into it. It got me thinking about how often I apologize for my behaviour in my day-to-day life.

I lived in the UK for nearly 20 years and perhaps this is a very British thing to do, but I can also guess that women do it more than men. It's like when you walk down the street and someone comes toward you, and you have to make a decision about whether to change your path. I read somewhere that women will make room for the other person more than men would. We are apologetic for the space we take up – "Sorry for making a fuss and disturbing anyone", "Sorry for taking your time", "Don't mind me" and so on. But finding your power entails becoming unapologetic – for your needs, for your desires, for the space you take up, for being loud, for having opinions, for being "difficult", "bossy", unliked, for putting yourself first, for wanting more, for expecting more and, ultimately, for being yourself.

I see so many brilliant women downplay their achievements and their success and their character. They flinch when given a compliment and deflect it. There is a general uncomfortableness about being praised, being in the limelight, taking credit – and this is probably a result of generations' worth of conditioning women to be humble, grateful and, above all, apologetic. The lack of confidence in too many women about our bodies, our relationships, our work, our parenting is mirrored with the excessive, sometimes unjustified, confidence of too many men. We walk around thinking our bodies are wrong so we need to fix them, or that we are not worth that promotion so we don't ask for it, or that we are not doing enough as mothers, while most men (and this is a generalization, I know) have a built-in sense of entitlement and are confident enough to ask for more, even when they don't always deserve it.

If we are going to reach our full potential we have to stop judging ourselves, and each other, so harshly. We have to be able to brag (yes, brag) about our abilities. We have to hype up other women and, essentially, we have to be supportive when other women hype themselves up. There is a tendency to dislike women who know their worth. We are often mistrusting – "Who does she think she is?" type of thing. I think the reason is that these women are not playing by the patriarchal rules and that can feel threatening and confusing. This is why women who are confident in themselves and know their worth often get torn down or vilified, sometimes by other women. But if we are to change this narrative we need to celebrate our successes and be each other's cheerleaders.

There's something profoundly liberating about women stepping into their unapologetic selves – it isn't about being harsh or disregarding others just for the sake of it, it's about honouring ourselves.

It's saying, "This is who I am, and I deserve to show up fully."

When we stop apologizing for existing as we are, we set an example for others, especially other women and girls, to do the same.

Be wild

There is something about our connection to mother nature, earth and the outdoors that lends itself to being free of the shackles of societal restraints. It's not about running like wolves (though I would love to do that and if you haven't read the book *Women Who Run With Wolves* by Clarissa Pinkola Estés then I strongly recommend you do),[45] and it's not about getting naked and rolling around in the mud (though that does sound like a lot of fun and it's 100 per cent on my bucket list) – it's really about tapping into the primal side of ourselves. For women this is sometimes hard to do because it doesn't sit well with how women are supposed to behave in our society.

This idea was summed up perfectly in the Chitta prologue in *Untamed* by Glennen Doyle (another must read).[46] which speaks about the captivity of women's bodies and spirits through a story about a cheetah kept captive in a zoo. When I read it for the first time it was as if I had finally understood that deep sense of longing for something I couldn't put into words. I don't know if you've ever had that feeling or not, but I very often feel like something inside me that has been held back, muted, and restricted is waiting to come out. Something wild. Something uncontrolled, unpredictable, scary – but not because it's bad, rather because it's limitless and free, and that by itself can be rather petrifying. But in a good way.

I haven't let go of this side of me completely just yet, although walking around my house without a bra on and my boobs swinging from side to side has felt rather wild and free in many ways. But it is without a doubt the next chapter of my life. I know that one of the ways to achieve this is by strengthening our connection to nature, spending more time outside, swimming in the ocean perhaps, planting vegetables, laying on the ground and gazing at the stars and, of course, dancing. One of my favourite practices is dancing to the sound of drums and if you haven't experienced it then please make sure you do.

Don't be led by fear

A good friend of mine told me recently she envied the fact I am not scared of trying new things and going after what I want. She said she wishes she could go away with her girlfriends for a few nights but is too scared to leave the kids behind in case something happens to them. She wishes she was brave enough to wear a swimming costume in summer and go to the beach but is too scared of what people might say about her body. She wishes she travelled more, took chances more, started that creative writing course she always wanted to take but she is scared that she wouldn't be good enough compared to other people. She said she was jealous of how fearless I was.

 I told her that while it may seem like I am not scared because I do all these things, it's not true. I am scared. Every time I leave the kids, every time I say yes to something new, every time I get on stage, every time I get on a plane, every time I do anything new, I worry. I am unsure. I wonder what people will think or say . . . But I do it anyway because I never want to regret not doing any of those things. And because I have learnt not to listen to fear when it whispers in my ear. I never want my fear to take away from my potential to live this life, right now, to the absolute fullest. So I do all these things while afraid. I have accepted that perhaps it's part of my process, and instead of trying to fight it, I take it with me for the ride. Some things get easier as you do them more often (like prancing around in a bikini with all my jiggly bits truly doesn't bother me any more), and some things don't (like flying). But I'm going to carry on doing them because I have found that the best things in life are beyond fear and I don't want to miss out on any of it – and neither should you.

Someone once told me when I was scared of doing something to focus on "one step at a time", and this is my advice to anyone who feels that starting something new or taking a chance is daunting. Don't focus on the whole picture; break it up into small bite size pieces and just focus on one bit at a time. Do not let fear lead you, otherwise you will never go anywhere or do anything.

Don't be good

My aunt in Ireland had postcards stuck onto the door in her downstairs loo which I loved looking at whenever we came to visit. My favourite read: "Good Girls Go To Heaven, Bad Girls Go Everywhere". Even as a 10 year old this quote made so much sense to me. I was the picture-perfect "good girl" and while that meant I got praise from my parents (especially my dad), it did feel limited, conditional and – how should I put it? – boring as hell. "Bad girls" had all the fun. They didn't care what people said about them, they were brash and bold and fearless and they paid a price for it. Society vilifies girls that don't obey the rules and as a child I felt like the price was too high to pay. What if boys don't respect me? What if my parents don't love me?

Well guess what? Being "likeable" and being "good" are overrated. Forget about it and tell your truest story. There will be someone out there who likes you for who and what you are; you don't need to try so hard.

As I've aged, and especially since turning 40, I have come to realize that being "good" (whatever that might mean) is overrated and that being "bad" is so much more fun. For me, being good meant playing the part I was expected to play – perfect daughter, good wife, excellent mother. It meant not rocking the boat, not questioning if any of that was truly what I wanted or if perhaps it was just something I did because everyone else did. Breaking away from the pressure and expectation to be good didn't mean becoming a horrible person who didn't care about anyone else, it simply meant putting myself back up on that priority list – at the very top. It meant going after things I wanted and listening to my inner voice more than listening to others. And most of all it meant stopping to care about what others think about me.

I can't stress enough how liberating that is.

You know, most of us walk around this world worried about what others might think or say about us and we try to be "good" so that we don't get judged. Two things have helped me care less: firstly, the fact that if people are going to judge, nothing you do or don't do will stop them. What I mean is that their judgement is usually more about them than it is about you and they are going to judge whether you like it or not, so you might as well give them good reason! Secondly, while it might seem like everyone is looking at what you're doing and just waiting to pounce, this is in fact not true. Most people are so self-involved, thinking about their own lives and own problems that they barely notice anyone else's.

In other words, people don't actually care about your cellulite.

As I age, and I don't think this is unique to me – I think many women go through this process – I shed more and more layers of "niceness". I don't care to be "good" if it means playing a role. I am good at heart in the sense that I try to do the right thing and I care about people, but I don't go out of my way to dismiss my own feelings, wants and desires just to make someone else feel validated. That's not my job.

And if that means I am "bad" then I'll take it.

We are strong

A few years ago, when my eldest was in Year Three, she took part in a school concert. She had a tiny solo playing her saxophone, which she had practised for and was so excited to perform in front of the whole school. We arrived early, sat at the front, and had our camera ready to capture her big moment.

She started playing, and my heart sank. She hit the wrong key, and it went downhill from there. For two minutes, she played completely off-key, screeching away until she was done. Everyone in the room knew she had made a mistake, but we all clapped, smiled, and gave her the thumbs-up. I could see she was holding back tears as she stood on stage for the rest of the show. When it was over, she ran straight to me and burst into tears.

There were lots of cuddles that evening and words of encouragement, but she felt so embarrassed. And I knew there was nothing I could do to fix it. That night, I turned to my husband Mike and said, "She's never playing sax again. This will be it for her. What a shame – she was getting really good at it. I just don't see her coming back from this."

The next day, the subject came up, and I cautiously asked her how she was feeling about playing the saxophone again. She turned to me and said, "I want to get a private tutor and work even harder on the saxophone so that I get really good and that never happens again."

My jaw dropped. I remember thinking, *Wow, what strength. If it were me, I would never have played the damn thing again.*

That day, my daughter taught me an important lesson about resilience. It's okay to get knocked down – it happens. Life throws challenges our way, and we can't avoid that. But we have more strength in us than we imagine.

I don't think enough women realize this. When people talk about strength, they often focus on physical strength – who can lift heavier weights, for example. And while that's impressive (and by the way, plenty of women do lift heavy physical loads), there's something even greater to be said about mental strength.

Women carry immense mental loads without breaking a sweat. Our families and communities rely on us. We reinvent ourselves multiple times throughout our lives. We get knocked down, and we get up – again and again.

Women are the most resilient people I know – the ones I'd want by my side in an emergency.

Don't ever forget how strong we are. And that we are even stronger together.

Do find a women's circle (and if you can't find one – create it!)

At the first women's circle I ever took part in, the facilitator asked us to place the palms of our hands in each other's palms. One hand would face up and the other face down. The person next to you would place their palm facing down on your palm that was facing up, and so on around the circle. It sort of created a chain, a receiving chain, going round and round in an infinitive circle.

This is exactly how I see female power – it's circular.

Female power emphasizes interconnectedness, balance and inclusivity, in contrast to the linear, top-to-bottom hierarchies of patriarchal structures. In this set-up the power is shared and it flows equally round and round in a circle. And if you think about it, this circular power aligns with so many things we see around us in nature, like the cycles of the moon, seasons of the year, and life itself. I often wonder what would happen if people sat in circles as standard – in classrooms, in board meetings, in parliament. Would that one seemingly little change in setting have the potential to change the world for the better?

We need our female friends to remind us who we are. That we are not in competition, that there is enough to go round.

We need our female friends to remind us that we are not selfish for tending to our needs and we are not a bad person for having boundaries. We need our female friends to tell us that whatever we are feeling is valid and deserves space and to be heard. We need our female friends to tell us that we are not crazy.

When women sit in a circle together it is a powerful act of healing and reclaiming the power that is, by definition, feminine. And if you add to that talking and sharing, music, drums, nature, laughter (and maybe chocolate) . . . well, then there is really no stopping us. It's a wonderful celebration of the power of women together.

Do gossip

Call up the girls.
Wake them up and tell them to come round.
Don't wait till tomorrow, don't say it's too late.
Don't claim there are more pressing things to do.
The dishes will be there later, someone else can feed the
    dog and the laundry can go fuck itself.

Call up the girls and get them over.
Revel in their humour and embrace their vulgarity.
Be silly, dance, gossip, stand on a table if you have to.
Share secrets, dreams, gin and as many carbs as you want,
And take off your bras, for fuck's sake.

Call the girls round before it's too late.
Before the years sneak past.
Before it's been too long since chatting till 4am about
    orgasms and cake.
And when your joints ache and memory flickers, you can
    look back and say, "We had fun, didn't we?"

NOTES

1. Caroline Criado Perez, *Invisible Women: Exposing Data Bias in a World Designed for Men*, Chatto & Windus, 2019
2. "gossip", OED.com
3. Esther Eidinow, *Envy, Poison, and Death*, Oxford Scholarship Online, 2015
4. Ashley D'Arcy, "The Feminist Origins of Gossip", The Good Trade, 14 August 2024, www.thegoodtrade.com/features/benefits-of-gossip/
5. Ibid.
6. "About History: The Scold's Bridle", Tastes of History, 2022, www.tastesofhistory.co.uk/post/about-history-the-scold-s-bridle
7. Yogita Limaye, "If We Can't Speak, Why Live?", 11 September 2024, BBC News, www.bbc.co.uk/news/articles/c20rq73p3z4o
8. Ashley D'Arcy, "The Feminist Origins of Gossip", The Good Trade, 14 August 2024, www.thegoodtrade.com/features/benefits-of-gossip/
9. "When Women Speak", Medium, 4 August 2016, MMJG, Medium.com
10. Louann Brizendine, M.D., *The Female Brain*, 2006
11. Tony Buon, "20,000/7,000 myth", LinkedIn, 2015, LinkedIn.com www.linkedin.com/pulse/do-women-talk-more-than-men-200007000-myth-tony-buon/.
12. "When Women Speak", Medium, 4 August 2016, MMJG, Medium.com
13. Olivia Gieger, "The Subtle Effects of Gender Disparities in the Classroom", The Amherst Student, 2018, https://amherststudent.amherst.edu/article/2018/03/20/subtle-effects-gender-disparities-classroom.html

14. Rebecca Sun, "Men Out-talk Women Almost Three To One In The Movies, Study Finds", The Hollywood Reporter, 2023, www.hollywoodreporter.com/movies/movie-news/hollywood-gender-study-women-1235342517/
15. "Wider Social Network May Help Women Live Longer", Harvard School of Public Health, 2019, https://hsph.harvard.edu/news/wider-social-network-may-help-women-live-longer/
16. "Coverture: The Word You Probably Don't Know But Should", Women's History, 2012, www.womenshistory.org/articles/coverture-word-you-probably-dont-know-should
17. "We Can't Believe These Shockingly Sexist Laws Existed In The UK", Stylist.com, 2017, www.stylist.co.uk/visible-women/law-lawyer-feminism-today-history-gender-pay-gap-abortion-equality/188525
18. OED reference
19. Jane Connor, PhD and Dian Killian, Ph D, *Connecting Across Differences*, PuddleDancer Press, 2012
20. "Violence against women", World Health Organization, www.who.int/news-room/fact-sheets/detail/violence-against-women
21. Brené Brown, "Listening to Shame", TED Talks, www.ted.com/talks/brene_brown_listening_to_shame
22. L Napilkoski, "Oppression and Women's History", Thoughtco.com, 2020, www.thoughtco.com/oppression-womens-history-definition-3528977
23. Ibid.
24. "Stress Relief From Laughter? It's No Joke", Mayo Clinic, www.mayoclinic.org/healthy-lifestyle/stress-management/in-depth/stress-relief/art-20044456
25. X Wu et al, "Association of screen exposure/sedentary behavior and precocious puberty/early puberty", *Sec. Pediatric Endocrinology*, 2024, 12, https://doi.org/10.3389/fped.2024.1447372
26. "Stress Relief From Laughter? It's No Joke", Mayo Clinic, www.mayoclinic.org/healthy-lifestyle/stress-management/in-depth/stress-relief/art-20044456

NOTES

27 A A Milne, *The House At Pooh Corner*, Methuen, 1928
28 Helen Foster, "Crones", Wellcome Collection, https://wellcomecollection.org/stories/crones
29 M Cohut, "The Controversy of 'Female Hysteria'", Medical News Today, 2020, www.medicalnewstoday.com/articles/the-controversy-of-female-hysteria
30 E Favilli and F Cavallo, *Good Night Stories for Rebel Girls*, Rebel Girls, 2016
31 Kerstin Lucker et al, *A History of The World with the Women Put Back In*, The History Press, 2019
32 Katy Hessel, *The Story of Art Without Men*, WW Norton & Company, 2023
33 Rosalind Miles, *The Women's History of the World*, HarperCollins, 2010
34 "Women's Circles Then and Now", Global Sisterhood, www.globalsisterhood.org/blog/womenscirclesthenandnow
35 Esther Perel, *Mating In Captivity*, Hodder & Stoughton 2006
36 Tova Leigh, *You Did What?*, Watkins, 2021
37 C Tasca et al, "Women and Hysteria in the History of Mental Health", *Clin Pract Epidemiol Ment Health*, 19 October 2012, 8:110–119. doi: 10.2174/1745017901208010110
38 *Masters of Sex* TV Series 2013–2016, based on 2009 book *Masters of Sex* by Thomas Maier
39 "Difficulty Reaching Orgasm a Common Problem for Women", 2024, The Science of Health/University Hospitals, www.uhhospitals.org/blog/articles/2024/06/difficulty-reaching-orgasm-a-common-problem-for-women
40 G Wade, "7 Benefits of Orgasms", health.com, 2024, www.health.com/sex/benefits-of-orgasm
41 "Infographic: The Price of Beauty", Department of Corrections Washington State, 2018, www.doc.wa.gov/docs/publications/infographics/100-PO031.htm
42 "Land Rights", Womankind Worldwide, www.womankind.org.uk/land-rights/

43 N J Simmonds, "Why The Superwoman Archetype is Damaging For Women", Medium, 2022, https://medium.com/inspire-the-mind/why-the-superwoman-archetype-is-damaging-for-women-fbc2f54306cc
44 "The Gift of the Good Enough Mother", Seleni.org, https://seleni.org/advice-support/2018/3/14/the-gift-of-the-good-enough-mother
45 Clarissa Pinkola Estes, *Women Who Run With The Wolves: Contacting the Power of the Wild Woman*, Rider, 2008
46 Glennon Doyle, *Untamed*, The Dial Press, 2020